EMPIRE BUILDERS

Visit empirebuildersgift.com/bonus to access valuable free gifts from each of the contributors

EMPIRE BUILDERS

11 WOMEN ENTREPRENEURS REVEAL THEIR SUCCESSES AND STRUGGLES ON THE WAY TO BUILDING THEIR EMPIRES

LISA DESPAIN

Copyright © 2018 by Lisa DeSpain
All Rights Reserved

ISBN: 978-0-578-42320-3

No part of this book may be reproduced or transmitted in any form or by any means, graphic, electronic, digital or mechanical, including photocopying, recording, taping, or by any information storage retrieval system, without the permission in writing from the author.

CONTENTS

Introduction ... 7

No More Quiet Desperation! ... 11
  Lisa DeSpain

Skip the Dark Side of Success ... 17
  Jennifer Dunham

From Confusion to Clarity ... 25
  Amanda Young

Do You Feel Like You're Not Enough or Are You Too Much? ... 37
  Cat Stancik

When Your Gut and Decisions Lead You Home ... 49
  Linda Poteet

The Castle ... 57
  Jen Levitz

Profit Is Your #1 Goal ... 65
  De'Lona "Dee" Moultrie

Empire Building Like a Nerd ... 73
  Amanda Goldman-Petri

Contribution ... 87
  Jodi Sodini

You Don't Have to See the Whole Staircase.
Just Take the First Step 95
   Vidya Ravi

Stressed as Hell to Aligned AF 103
   Katrina Hubbard

Conclusion 119

INTRODUCTION

"Asking a millionaire for their secret to success is like looking at a journey of 1,000 miles and asking which step was the most important. They're all important."

—Jason Seidell, QuikTrip Corporation

It's true, isn't it? We all search for the magic bullet to success. We are drawn in by gurus and experts who all claim to have the magic bullet. Each of these experts has perfected *their* system for success, usually after years and years of hard work. Those systems may not work for you, or they may be useful tools you add to your roadmap to personal success. It's up to each of us to learn everything we can and implement what makes sense for our business. Whether you're currently an entrepreneur or wish to be one, the more you're in business, the more you realize that success is built on years and years of small habits and activities.

The women entrepreneurs you'll meet in this book are incredible forces for good in their industries. I've compiled their stories to encourage you and to show you what's possible. When I started my first business, it was hard to find great female role models. More than anything, I wanted to know the stories of other women who had "made it" on their own terms, who thought so much bigger than just the 9-to-5. I wanted to know *Empire Builders*. Instead of having female role models and some sort of blueprint for success, I ended up just building according to my own vision. And the truth?

I thought smaller than I should. I grew slowly and limited myself for no good reason. When we have great role models, we know what's possible. We have something to aim for, and an example to follow when things go wrong in our businesses. We can be encouraged, knowing that our resolve will be tested as part of the process. I hope this book can help you dream bigger and push through obstacles, too.

In compiling this book, I noticed some clear patterns. None of us has had it easy, either in our personal lives or our businesses. *None* of our first businesses became an overnight success. Many of us are on our third business, having closed one or more businesses or dissolved partnerships in our past. In all that struggle, the lessons we've learned have helped us build business number three, four, or ten in a more informed way. We live by the quote, "If at first you don't succeed, try, try again."

Another thing I've learned about entrepreneurs is that we've never really arrived. There will always be more we can do: more clients we can serve, more products and services we can offer, and more revenue and profit we can make. Each entrepreneur you'll read about is working on their next business goal. We tend to set the next target, even before we've properly celebrated the last milestone we reached. It's just what we do. We crave momentum and results.

Because we work from home, we tend to be isolated unless we make it a point to connect with others, whether in person or online. Some of us are introverted and struggle to pick up the phone. Most have pushed past their tendency to disconnect and have made their times of extroversion really count, like for sales calls, business or client retreats, affiliate opportunities, speaking engagements, or trainings.

If you're wondering if becoming an entrepreneur is right for you, or if you've been in business for some time and are ready to dream bigger, this book is for you. The writers in this book have shared their struggles and successes. They're from widely different

INTRODUCTION

backgrounds, locations, ethnicities, and talents. You'll see your story in some of theirs, and be encouraged by seeing how they overcame challenges in their lives. Let them encourage you as you become an Empire Builder!

Be sure to visit empirebuildersgift.com/bonus to access valuable free gifts from each of the contributors.

LISA DESPAIN

NO MORE QUIET DESPERATION!

"Most men lead lives of quiet desperation and go to the grave with the song still in them."

—Henry David Thoreau

This quote stirs something in me that says, "Not me!" I can't think of anything more depressing than to die without having fulfilled one's purpose. I wonder if Thoreau thought of women at all when he wrote this quote. If *men* weren't living their full potential in his day, weren't women able to live even less of their potential?

Even though I'm not quite done yet, today I believe I'm closer to fulfilling my purpose than any other point in my life. In my company, Book 2 Bestseller, I help entrepreneurs write and publish their books to quickly establish them as an authority in their industry.

Being a Kid

My mom had two miscarriages before she had me and one after. I always knew I was wanted and loved. We traveled quite a bit when I was little because my dad worked for Phillips 66. When I was just eighteen months old, we moved to Lagos, Nigeria, where we lived for a year-and-a-half. We moved back to Bartlesville,

Oklahoma where my sister, Laura, was born. Then we moved to Bogotá, Colombia, where I went to kindergarten and where my other sister, Erica, was born. Then we moved back to Bartlesville (the then-headquarters of Phillips) where we stayed for the next twelve years.

> *I was, and am, a nerd, and I'm finally proud of it!*

Growing up in Bartlesville was unique, but boring. For a small town, it had a relatively high average income because of the Phillips 66 crowd. I don't know if it is common for other small towns in the eighties, but there was nothing for kids to do, especially teenagers. I was sheltered. I only found out later that some of the popular kids had been into drugs and partying on the weekends. I never would have fit in with that crowd. I was, and am, a nerd, and I'm finally proud of it!

In high school, one of my three jobs was working at the public library. I especially enjoyed doing programming in the children's room, and working at the main circulation desk was fun, too.

College, Alcohol, and Smoking

The summer before college, my dad took me on a 16-day tour of Europe. We visited West Germany, Austria, Switzerland, France, and Italy. What an amazing adventure! I drank bitter German beer in Lucerne, learned how to yodel, and sang Edelweiss, the Austrian national anthem (you might recognize it from *Sound of Music*) at a beautiful vineyard in the mountains. This was also the first time I got drunk.

That year, I started my freshman year at the University of Tulsa. Going to college was a revelation. I no longer had anyone telling me what to do. It was all up to me. Within the first week of my freshman year, I had picked up drinking and smoking. While drinking may have been an inevitable bad habit, smoking was something I started just to fit in with people in the dorm. Before long, I was partying every weekend, waking up late, and pulling too many all-nighters, trying to keep up with my schoolwork.

Mommy!

My husband and I met in January before I started my senior year of college. We married in May, already pregnant with our first daughter, Nicole, who was born in November. I finished out my degree that December with a double major in political science and international studies and finished in three-and-a-half years, with a newborn.

Getting a job was difficult. I don't know if it was because I was in a different place than most of the people I graduated with or if it was a difficult job market for everyone in 1993. I found a job at the University, working in the continuing education department.

When my daughter was eighteen months old, I decided to leave TU to stay home with her, so I foolishly started a home day care. This helped me realize that I like my own kids, but not always everyone else's, and certainly not every day all the time. That little business closed in about a week, with the only permanent feature being Play-Doh mashed into the carpet.

> *I like my own kids, but not always everyone else's.*

We discovered we were pregnant with my son, Nathan, and he was born a few days before I turned twenty-five, in January 1997. With two kids under four, this started a short period of time when I stayed home with them and didn't work outside the home.

God Tricked Me

In 1998, I started working with a temp agency, and they placed me at a Christian publishing company based in Tulsa. I had seen some weird sounding classified ads that started something like this: "Spirit-filled Christian publishing company in CityPlex towers seeks…" I thought, *That's a bunch of weirdos in the clouds.* I never would have applied there on my own, but that's exactly where the temp agency sent me. Looking back, this was a God thing. I had found my people.

Because I was a temp, the publishing company had no obligation to hire me. I worked for the sales team, and they'd never had a temp who could keep up with the work, had a great attitude all the time, and who could spell. (In college, I had almost enough credits to graduate with an English degree, so yeah, I could spell.) The sales team wanted to keep me, but I had made the mistake of telling human resources that I wasn't sure if I believed everything they believed. The door was shut.

The sales team cornered the president of the company one day at lunch. I had been a little put out that they didn't take me to lunch, too, but they had a plan. Each one of them went around the table and pleaded my case. He relented, and that started my sixteen-year career with the company.

> *I had found my people.*

I've always loved books. I was the kid who stayed up all night to finish a book, reading with a flashlight under the covers, and bleary-eyed in the morning. I read every one of the *Little House on the Prairie* books multiple times. I was an early adopter of more adult fiction, back when YA fiction wasn't really a thing.

While I was at the company, I learned everything about publishing, from warehousing and distribution to web design and database management. I also learned about editing, book layout for print, and how to identify a bestselling cover. In the time I was there, I helped to implement three massive system software changes. I even took the company's backlist books and converted them all to ebooks.

Also during this time, I finally stopped drinking. I had always been able to stop drinking and smoking when I was pregnant. In fact, I stopped smoking for good when I discovered I was pregnant with Nathan. But drinking still had a hold on me, and it wouldn't be until I became spiritually strong that I could break it for good. I had joined a multi-level marketing company and started doing positive affirmations because I really wanted to do well with the company. I grew stronger and stronger, and one New Year's Day, I quit drinking, and haven't had a drink since. I firmly believe I was delivered from addiction. I attended no meetings and didn't tell a soul—after all, I worked at a Christian publishing company. I don't know to this day if they would have fired me if they had known I was a closet drinker, who would frequently show up for work with a hangover.

I used the skills I learned at the publishing company to launch my ebook conversion company. Over the course of several years, my team and I hand-coded over 2,000 ebooks and helped the authors get them ready for sale. I also helped some of those authors prepare their books for print. A few years later, I entered a partnership with an established self-publishing company, but soon realized I prefer being "in charge" and dissolved my share in the company.

Where I'm Going

My favorite people are entrepreneurs, and my favorite part of the publishing process is the story. Stories can take on many forms. A brand story connects the company to potential clients, while a signature book details the entrepreneur's system (their client transformation process) to the reader. At the highest, most comprehensive level, story can document the company's processes, systems, and people in the form of an operations manual or set of standard operating procedures. I love all of it, and I specialize in fun, easy ways for business owners and entrepreneurs to communicate their stories, so they can build legacies that last.

So, tell me *your* story!

EMPIRE BUILDER

LISA DESPAIN

*L*isa DeSpain is the owner of Systems for Scaling, a service that helps businesses build standard operating procedures to scale operations, delegate effectively, franchise, or sell. With a background in system implementation, operations, and staff training, Lisa understands large-scale business systems and how they relate to individual processes and people.

To access Lisa's gift, go to empirebuildersgift.com/bonus.

Jennifer Dunham

SKIP THE DARK SIDE OF SUCCESS

"Ask yourself if what you're doing today is getting you closer to where you want to be tomorrow."

—Unknown

Ever have a bad morning? You spill coffee down the front of yourself as you're rushing out the door. You can't remember if you shut the garage door when you left the house. Your colleague quietly informs you that you are wearing one black shoe and one navy shoe right as you are about to start a big presentation. (That last one didn't happen to me but to a friend...really! I swear.)

It's only 9AM and you're already wondering...Could anything more go wrong?!

Can you relate?

Imagine that bad day feeling, but on steroids. I was having a bad summer.

> *Imagine that bad day feeling, but on steroids.*

I was t-boned in an intersection by a drunk driver who ran a red light at over 80 mph. My husband and I, after attempting counseling, were going through a divorce. And I was on the receiving end of those dreaded words, "You have cancer."

WTF. Why me?!

I was lost. Have you heard the saying, "You have a breakdown just before a breakthrough?" I knew a change was coming...but what?

I sat eating pizza and drinking a glass of wine in a restaurant... alone. (Being alone can be good sometimes.)

I pulled out my journal and decided to write the answer to this question: What Would I Do If I Won the Lottery?

After paying off my debt, mortgages, taking care of my parents, traveling the world, and adding a few more dozen shoes to my growing shoe collection, the really good stuff started to show up.

The last line read...Teach Others the Passion of Living.

Not long after I wrote those words, I met my now second husband. He bought me a camera at Christmas and I ran full steam ahead into showing others the passion of living through photographs...and opened my photography studio.

Did I mention that this was a side hustle? I already owned and operated a small IT firm.

I'm one of "those" entrepreneurs: Multi-talented. Multi-passionate. Forever recovering perfectionist and workaholic.

What can I say...been that way my whole life.

I work hard.

What Would I Do If I Won the Lottery?

My grandfather taught me: "Go to school, work hard, save up and plan for the future with your family."

I had no idea what I wanted to study in college, but I had to check a box, so I selected Computer Science. Why you ask? Why not?

I grew up in a small town and had only one small computer course in high school, but it sounded fun. I would be a full-time student the rest of my life if I could. I really enjoyed most subjects.

I graduated valedictorian from high school. I graduated Summa Cum Laude (with Honors) with a B.S. in computer science and minor in mathematics. I went on to grad school to get an M.S. in computer science, focusing on artificial intelligence (A.I.), analysis of algorithms, and psychology.

I was working on a D.O.D. and N.A.S.A. contract in grad school. *YAWN*. You would fall asleep if I told you the title of my thesis.

Fast forward several years.

I own a successful Information Technology firm and now an award-winning photography studio.

My photography studio was becoming one of the top studios in my area and known as one of the most expensive (which I took as great compliment).

> *There is a dark side to success.*

All my hard work was paying off.

Or was it?

What my grandfather didn't teach me is that drive and success often breed the need to work even harder and create more success. *There is a dark side to success.*

The competitive nature in me made me compete against myself. I didn't necessarily want more money. I lived comfortably, and I was smart with money. But pride? Well, pride a is deadly sin. There's a reason why they consider it to be the deadliest.

It can kill you. (remember that Bad Summer story I shared?)

My (2nd) husband and I were arguing all the time. He hated where we lived. I hated how he didn't help around the house. He hated how much I worked. I hated how we never did anything together any more. Back and forth it went.

I was working too much. My health and fitness were suffering. Obviously, my relationship was suffering.

Something's gotta give. Cause I was about to give up.

It's got to be easier than this!

One evening and one conversation made the entire difference in the trajectory of my career.

"What are we waiting for?" I asked my husband. We had always talked about living on some acreage when we retire.

...Someday.

That night, my husband and I decided to move out of the 'burbs and onto a small five-acre chicken farm. We agreed it was doable so long as it was within commuting distance of our clients.

Seven days later, we found the house of our dreams. Thirty days later, we moved.

> *If something's not working... change it. Simple, right?*

There are seven days in a week and "Someday" is not one of them. It's a mantra I share with my clients all the time now.

It saved my life. It saved my marriage. It propelled my career and success to an entirely different level.

It made me realize that if something's not working... change it. Simple, right?

Yes, that simple.

Change is good.

I was happier. Life and work became easier. It was noticeable.

My friends joked and asked, "What are you growing out on your farm, Jennifer?"

They wanted to know what I was taking. No, it's not what you are thinking!

I told them the secret was "drinking coffee with my chickens every morning."

The computer science A.I. geek in me wanted to figure out what was "it" that really was making the difference.

Repetition.

Automation.

Daily happiness.

Making better choices with my time.

I'm good at analyzing algorithms...and this includes how to best spend my time and how to streamline tasks to get more done in less time.

Remember the 80/20 rule? 80% of your clients won't even notice the last 20% effort you put in. 20% of the time spent on a certain area of a business creates 80% of that business' results.

I scaled way back on my photography work. I'm using "scaled back" loosely. I worked myself out of my photography company. Today, I choose not to shoot much anymore at all, unless it's for a very good friend or past client.

Instead I spend weekends at home, with my husband and chickens and our two cats, Zipper and Velcro.

I founded a new business, HappinessMatters.com, but this time, I was bound and determined to share with others how to build and grow businesses in a smart way.

I could share my expertise with others to help them find their unique balance, make more money by doing less, and enjoy their path to making millions.

I call myself a Time, Money and Happiness Matters expert. These are just 3 components in my Profitable Lifestyle Formula™ but they are the most important.

Master your time.
Master your money.
Master your happiness.
You must master all 3.

Many people would like to tell you that "Happiness can't be bought." They're full of crap.

> *Master your time. Master your money. Master your happiness.*

If you don't have enough money, you can't pay the rent. It affects your health, your relationships, and your well-being.

And to make consistent money…while enjoying your life… you must use your time in the wisest way.

You *can* be smarter about your time, your money, and yes, even your happiness.

By leveraging the power of Tiny Habits, you can get more done in less time. You can focus on what makes you money. And I swear by my method of being happier in less than five minutes a day.

My approach with my clients is rooted in my information Technology background. I'm a huge believer in automation, habits, repeatable processes, and streamlining to reduce overwhelm so you can focus on what matters most.

You will hear me say, "Structure equals Freedom."

I believe it so much that I became certified as a Tiny Habits coach, and I'm a certified cash injection specialist.

> *You can break through those chains and create your profitable lifestyle.*

You don't have to feel chained to your desk.

You don't have to feel chained to your success.

You can break through those chains and create your profitable lifestyle.

I help driven professionals learn how to not only love their success and career but also fully love their lives.

I recommend you evaluate, and evaluate often, if your life needs a course correction. We just too easily get stuck in our comfort zones. Change is good.

Now I have chicken shit on my boots and my clothes are dusty most days. I still successfully operate multiple businesses. But…

I love my life.

EMPIRE BUILDER

JENNIFER DUNHAM

As a Time, Money and Happiness lifestyle coach, Jennifer helps driven professionals learn how love their success and career and fully love their lives.

Jennifer's approach is rooted in her IT background. She's a huge believer in automation, habits, repeatable processes and streamlining to reduce overwhelm so you can focus on what matters most. She teaches her clients how to find more time, so they can make more money and increase their happiness.

Jennifer is a motivational speaker. Audiences love Jennifer's relatable stories and specific strategies that they can use right away to help them grow and scale their business in a way that aligns with their desired lifestyle and values.

Jennifer is a cancer survivor. She knows "Life Is Short" and she will tell it to you like it is.

When Jennifer isn't working, you will find her hiking with her hubby, playing with their kitties Zipper and Velcro, or tending to their small chicken farm in the Sierra foothills in Northern California.

To access Jennifer's gift, go to empirebuildersgift.com/bonus.

AMANDA YOUNG

FROM CONFUSION TO CLARITY

We've all heard of people having a so-called mid-life crisis. I joke that mine was a quarter-life crisis and came at age 23, then kept coming again and again at age 25, 27, and 32. By age 30 I could list around 30 different jobs I'd had from my teenage years to 35. Those were the good old days, when Oprah Winfrey was pushing the search for our passions and I was desperately on the hunt. I sought advice from every source available to me during those times: self-help books, motivational speakers, mentors, co-workers, friends in other industries, and anyone who would listen. My goal was to find my passion, and then figure out how to make money doing it. Fearing that I couldn't do it alone, I believed that I didn't know how to get started. After all, by the time I reached 32, I had a husband, two kids, and a mortgage to pay. The American dream was in motion and I was well on my way to the single-family home with a white picket fence and a golden retriever. That's what I was supposed to do to be happy, right? Go to school, get a good

> *That's what I was supposed to do to be happy, right?*

job, make money, buy a house, have kids… and then what? Pay for college, weddings, retirement, and eventually get to spoil grandchildren? I was stuck on the "get a good job part" and the rest of it just sounded expensive and exhausting.

I was miserable.

> *My panic attacks were so bad that my vision would fade into blackness.*

It felt like my bosses didn't appreciate me, my talents weren't being used, I wasn't fulfilled by any of my jobs, the limitations of bureaucracy were holding back my performance, and promotions were not happening fast enough or fitting into my mentality of "I'm amazing so why can't you just let me be in charge already."

Rock bottom for me was the six-month period in my life when I had to stop driving because my panic attacks were so bad that my vision would fade into blackness. I was terrified of causing an accident and gravely injuring someone. Jobs that promised flexibility and opportunity didn't match my expectations, and the physical toll they were taking on my health were no longer worth the trouble. Out of desperation, I again switched jobs after a short six-month stint at a charter school. Out of one rough situation, I quickly landed into another. I was buying weddings rings from divorced women for pennies on the dollar, which was the equivalent of selling my soul to the devil. On the already depressing anniversary of September 11th, for the very first time in my life, I was fired. Weirdly, it was one of the happiest days of my life since it meant I got out of that job, qualified for unemployment, and would be able to figure out my next steps. Things had to get better.

Confusion

As I searched for jobs that would value my talents, be relevant to my education level and experience, pay me what I was "worth," and allow me the flexibility to be with my kids more than any other caregiver in their lives, I realized that I wasn't a very good employee. Ambition, stubbornness, confidence, intolerance of inefficiencies, determination, and a very strong desire to change the world weren't always welcome in the typical workplace and were often seen as threatening. There was more for me and it was my job to figure out what "more" really was.

I began the real search: to find myself, my soul's calling, my passion, my superpowers, and my place in this world. Until this point, as with most things in my life, I assumed that all the advice I'd been told *must* be high-quality because I'd been taught to listen to my teachers and respect my elders. As the child of an educator, education was of utmost importance growing up, and I understood learning to be a never-ending process that would always lead me to the right answers. The line right there is key—learning would always lead me to the *right* answers. The art of discerning which of the knowledge being presented to me was "good" or "bad" wasn't ever an issue. Throughout my life, I'd been educated by high-quality teachers in top-ranked schools, using reference materials and sources that were far superior to the unverified quality of opinions on the Internet. The underlying assumption was that everything I'd been taught in my life was "right" and there was no reason to question any of it. If I followed the rules, got good grades, and listened to my elders, I'd be successful.

> *There was more for me and it was my job to figure out what "more" really was.*

In my search for a job, I was introduced to an older gentleman in the banking industry. His job was business development for an accounting firm, so he was connected with the most influential and powerful men in the city. Since he was older than me, clearly more knowledgeable, and obviously far more wealthy and well-off than I was, I took everything he said as complete truth (just as I had with countless other bosses in my career). When he insisted I have a chocolate croissant and a scone for breakfast, I agreed, despite having a sensitivity to gluten that caused a massive headache when I consumed any foods made with flour. I wanted to be the good girl. I wanted to please him and show him that I, too, could be successful. Above all, I wanted to be polite. Somehow, that also meant that I needed to eat the croissant and scone to prove that I could measure up.

> *I no longer needed to subscribe to the idea that everyone knew better than I did.*

I ate every bite of the glutinously delicious breakfast and found myself in excessive pain just hours later, wondering why I was such a fool. It was a painful lesson, but eventually I realized that not all advice was good, gluten was no longer a "maybe just this once" but instead a strict "no," and I no longer needed to subscribe to the idea that everyone knew better than I did. After all, what good was all that knowledge if I didn't know when, where, why, and how to apply all that I'd learned? There's a point in life when the student must shift, start making decisions for themselves, and become a teacher. It was time for me to step out and start my own business.

Early on, I picked up a few side projects and tried to figure out how to become a consultant, freelancer, or entrepreneur—and which of those names defined me as a solo business owner trying to make money doing something that helped others. Scouring hundreds of articles, websites, training classes for women entrepreneurs, and free downloads promising dreamy results left me super confused by conflicting advice with even less clarity than when I started.

Without business cards or a website, I wasn't sure how to charge people for my time or my services, and I didn't really know what to say or how to find clients. Secretly I wished someone would walk me through the whole process of entrepreneurship so that I didn't waste time and money taking the wrong actions and becoming a failed business statistic.

> *Entrepreneurship is an inside job and one that completely changes the way you view your world.*

Support

It's said that when the student is ready, the teacher appears. In my quest for more information, guidance along my path, and a way forward, I bought an online program from a business coach, went to her coaching retreat, and signed up to work with her for a year to lay out the foundation for my business. That was when I started getting to know myself, understanding my strengths, and figuring out what I loved to do. A large part of that process was learning about my intuition, how to trust my gut and follow the signs the Universe was leaving for me as breadcrumbs to my future.

I'd love to say that I was an instant success, but that's just what many programs want you to believe will happen these days. They are selling formulas, strategies, and programs guaranteed to make you successful quickly. What they don't explain is that the results aren't always typical and are rarely sustainable. There isn't a magic pill that makes you successful. It's a process that takes time, effort, and a clear sense of direction.

Once I started to gain clarity around what I wanted and who I was meant to serve, I won new clients, drafted contracts, received payments, designed a new logo, printed business cards, built my website, and technically was in business as a copywriter and marketing consultant. At that point, I was pretty sure that I just needed to rinse and repeat whatever I had done previously to find clients, take more actions toward my six-figure income goal, and meet enough people to make that happen. What I didn't understand, despite all the programs I invested in, the sales/speaking/writing coaches I hired, and the hours spent networking, blogging, writing, reading, and trying to find more clients, was that entrepreneurship is really an inside job and one that completely changes the way you view your world.

> *It takes a strong support team to raise a successful and sustainable business.*

Beyond investing time, effort, and money into your business, you will need to take aligned action toward your goals with a willingness to face your fears, identify the stories blocking you from your success, and get out of your own way so that you can finally allow yourself to shine. That's not something that happens overnight but it will happen through the support of coaches, mentors, advisors, and friends who have gone before you. They can listen to your situation and reflect what's happening back to you in a way that allows you to see your next steps and continue moving forward. Don't assume you're meant to struggle on this journey alone. The proverb, "It takes a village to raise a child" describes entrepreneurship, too. It takes a strong support team to raise a successful and sustainable business.

Misunderstanding

To be successful, I believed that I had to go after what I wanted, work hard for the money, put in my time, take any business that came to me, cast a wide net so that I had more chances to catch everything, work a room while networking to make sure I didn't miss any opportunities, and convince clients to work with me. The amount of pressure to perform, get everything right, and have a perfect business destined to succeed kept me motivated for the first couple of years until I realized I was exhausted, my results were limited, and my business wasn't sustainable. My income varied dramatically from month to month and I had no system to consistently attract new clients.

When we embark on the path of entrepreneurship, we have high hopes that clients will find us easily, we'll spend more time doing what we love, and we'll make good money doing it. We see successful business owners portrayed in the media as examples of the American Dream and what's possible with hard work, determination, and some elbow grease. What they don't explain in these stories is that all entrepreneurs *aren't* made equal. Some of us are heart-centered and aren't in the business just to make money. We want to make a difference, change the world, improve the lives of those around us, and genuinely help others while making money. Having tried the traditional marketing methods, we've followed the rules we've been given as standard ways of getting clients to buy from us. If we fail to have true, lasting success, we feel defeated, become discouraged, and wonder what we're doing wrong. After all, we listened to advice from the experts, did what they told us to do, and yet, we still lack the fulfillment we set out for in the beginning.

> *Some of us are heart-centered and aren't in the business just to make money.*

Temptation begs us to give up, quit, leave entrepreneurship for those with thicker skin and deeper pockets. The fearful voices in our heads encourage us to go back and get a job, when they aren't busy berating us for a myriad of reasons—not being good enough, worthy of success, qualified to help, ready to do the job, smart enough, etc.

We often have so much conflicting advice that we no longer know who to trust, what to believe, or what step to take next. Paralysis sets in and we become overwhelmed by our business. Our confidence becomes shaken, desperation kicks in, and soon our business is failing, and, despite our best efforts, we aren't sure why because we've been following everyone else's advice all along.

And that, my friends, is the problem.

Clarity

The first step in successfully navigating the entrepreneurial journey is to understand we have all the answers inside of us. We often need the support of trained coaches, mentors, or guides to help us discover it, follow it, and use it to our advantage, but the answers we need are always within us. That's not to say you have permission now to emotionally beat yourself up because you haven't figured out how to be successful yet. It does mean you know more than you're admitting to in the moment because fears, past beliefs, and other unconscious factors hold you back and hide the answers from you. That creates confusion and inaction.

> *We have all the answers inside of us.*

We are so restricted by the conflicting advice we've been given, the rules we've been told to follow, and the formulas for success that we become paralyzed by our fears and do nothing. When you are willing to face your fears, reframe the beliefs that no longer serve you, and take the very next step toward what you want, you can get into the flow and allow great things to happen.

Clarity comes once you do the deeper work to identify the fears stopping you, clear out the beliefs that used to protect you but now inhibit you, and focus on action steps to move you forward. When you learn to tap into your intuition, have fun in your business, be present in this very moment, fully embrace your own personality, be of service to others, and allow your talents to really shine, you gain the clarity you need to create consistent and continued success.

When you chase your dreams, they keep running, like a dog escaping the restraints of his leash. The easiest way to "catch" him is to get him to come to you by running away from him. The counter-intuitive actions that aren't taught in corporate jobs or business schools will point us to our ultimate success. Instead of convincing clients to work with us, we learn to shine brightly and become the sun that attracts the clients who need our warmth. When you release the beliefs causing you to stay in confusion, you allow clarity to replace the chaos. Then you can align with your true calling and allow your dreams to come to you.

> *Learn to shine brightly and become the sun that attracts the clients who need your warmth.*

Possibility

By managing our energy, focusing on the results we want, taking inspired action toward our goals, getting the support we need, listening to our intuition, and being our authentic selves, we have the power to create the business, success, and abundance beyond our wildest dreams. You must get curious about what's possible and seek more of what you love. It might be counter to what you have been taught in life thus far, but curiosity will serve you well.

A struggling photographer in Portland, Oregon stumbled upon my book, *Finding Clarity: Design A Business You Love and Simplify Your Marketing*. Any former passion for her photography business was gone as she attracted the wrong clients asking for the wrong type of work, at rates that weren't worth her time, with little hope for improvement in her near future. Together, we identified her interests and superpowers. She had a love of fashion, travel, photography, and connecting with others on a deeper level. After some digging, she realized that she had a true passion for helping women recover from heartbreak. Years ago, she had suffered a devastating breakup which left her lost, reclusive, and distant from everything she used to love. Her journey led her on a European travel adventure of self-discovery and healing unlike anything else she had tried. It was that extraordinary travel experience that inspired her to start a company arranging travel to help women get their sparkle back. After just six months of coaching, she got the support and clarity she needed to be fully in alignment with her purpose and her soul's calling. She knows who she is, what she wants, who her ideal clients are, what they need, and what will serve them best. By knowing where to find them, and how to speak with them, she easily attracted her first client by simply connecting with an old friend. Now she's eager to go to work in her business, excited to meet new people, and has launched an amazing website to beautifully communicate the value she provides women during some of the most difficult moments of their lives.

Get curious about what's possible and seek more of what you love.

By getting clear on who she is, what she really wanted, and understanding the previous beliefs that were holding her back from her true calling and lasting success, she was able to tap into her intuition. She designed a business she really loves while serving others in a beautiful way. As she connected with her heart, she uncovered the beliefs that were holding her back and not serving her nor allowing her to serve her clients.

You can have this same level of success. Businesses can be built with ease and grace or struggle and hardship. You can worry that you don't have a website and a logo, or you can ask prospective clients how you can help them and get paid to do what you love. You can fret over having systems in place, or you can figure things out along the way while taking imperfect action and learning to love every step of the process no matter how ugly it may be. The best part of entrepreneurship is that you get to choose your path. Once you do, be sure to commit fully, be aware of the mindset traps that will try to dismantle your success, and continue to take deliberate, inspired actions toward your dreams on a consistent basis for consistently amazing results.

> *Businesses can be built with ease and grace or struggle and hardship.*

You already have all the answers you need inside of you. Follow your heart, get the support you need early on to avoid wasting your time and money chasing the wrong things, and design your business to be of service to the clients who need you most. They are waiting for you right now, asking for your help. Are you willing to answer their call?

EMPIRE BUILDER

AMANDA YOUNG

Amanda H. Young, MBA, bestselling author of *Finding Clarity: Design a Business You Love and Simplify Your Marketing*, is known for helping creative entrepreneurs find the clarity they need to define their ideal clients, design a business they love, and manage their energy while enjoying the freedom of running a successful business. She provides much-needed focus and clarity to ambitious business owners who have unique talents to share with the world. By cutting through the clutter and getting to the core of her clients' strengths and capabilities, Amanda aligns the services they provide with the people they are meant to serve and simplifies their message and marketing in a way that attracts clients effortlessly. Contact her at Amanda@SimplifyYourMarketing.com.

To access Amanda's gift, go to empirebuildersgift.com/bonus.

CAT STANCIK

DO YOU FEEL LIKE YOU'RE NOT ENOUGH OR ARE YOU TOO MUCH?

I was born not enough.

With five sisters, I always fell short in the comparison game—despite being the tallest (my only virtue at the time). Reinforced by my parents, teachers, and even my own sisters... why had I been born this way?

Why was it so hard to breathe and take up space?

Growing up sucked.

Now don't get me wrong, this isn't a sob story about all the drama and terrible things that happened to me. Those things happened... terrible, horrible things. Things I thought were my fault, or that I somehow justified as being ok. This story is about the other side of that experience.

> *I was born fierce, with a purpose, and unquenching thirst to make an impact.*

I was also born fierce, with a purpose, and unquenching thirst to make an impact in the world.

My "weaknesses" growing up—being too loud, too emotional, too hungry—are now my strengths. My too-muchness is what's making my fortune today. I was able to turn what others saw as annoying, aggressive, and demanding, into determination, drive, and confidence.

How did I do it?

There are three critical moments that helped propel me to where I am today. Moments that helped me turn away from victim into victor!

One—I Was Helped

> *I was seeking comfort, but the only comfort I knew came from food.*

There are always low points in life… but the lowest ones stay with us.

One of these moments was when I was 22-years-old, living in a windowless basement apartment, friendless, and stuck in a dead-end job I hated (and sucked at). I couldn't afford the internet, so I'd drive to the local library to get online, to look for love in all the wrong places. I was desperately seeking human interaction… just wanting a friend and some love… because didn't I deserve something?

When I was looking for love, I was seeking comfort, but the only comfort I knew came from food.

I keenly remember not being able to afford much, and since I had to feed my emotions, I headed to the local Wal-Mart and bought a $2 frozen apple pie. I came home, heated it up, and ate the whole thing in one sitting, all on my own.

I remember not being hungry… but almost force feeding myself. If I kept eating, all I had to feel was the discomfort of my bloating belly, not my emotional pain.

Food had been a comfort my whole life, but at 320lbs, I had lost control. In fact, the only thing I thought I could control was what I ate, and I was eating for a whole life of unfair.

My mom saw my pain, my struggle, and I know inside she felt my pain. Pain of a lifetime of rejection and just wanting to fit in.

Pain from never measuring up and falling short. Pain of wanting a better life, and not knowing how to get it.

That's when she helped me in her own way. She helped me see the life I was living and gave me the gift of life a second time.

She helped me with scheduling and going through gastric bypass.

I'd struggled my entire life with my weight. I was the only one of my sisters who had ever been chubby (see the comparison game going on here)—and yes, my parents fucked up with how they handled it... adding to my inability to manage my emotions and struggles. It was no wonder I turned to food for comfort. But it's not about that anymore... this is *my* Hero's Journey after all!

So, at 23, I did what I considered giving up. I moved back in with my mom—a clear sign of failure—to have what I believed was my last chance at a happy life. I had gastric bypass. At 320 pounds, and a lifetime of diets and magic bullet solutions, I needed to be resuscitated.

I was born again.

Six months later, I found myself earning the most I ever had. $40,000 at the time was a lot. I made a down payment on my first condo in DC!

Often, it's not that people aren't *willing* to help; we must also *allow* ourselves to be helped.

I've said it before—but will say it again. Thank you, Mom <3!

> **Wasn't being skinny supposed to fix everything?**

Two—I Found Value

Now life was supposed to be moving along, right? I was a svelte size eight—holy shit! I was having fun for the first time in my life, but I still wasn't happy.

What the hell? Wasn't being skinny supposed to fix everything? Wasn't that going to make life easier? I would find love, because I was hot... there were no excuses now!

Well, apparently that's not how it works. Fuck.

There I was again, but this time what I thought was my problem—being fat—was solved, and I still wasn't being swept up off my feet by my prince charming (thanks, Disney).

The other thing I used to do was escape into movies (and I still do this, but I'll add books in too now). You know how you can read or watch something, and maybe even see it multiple times, but then something new stands out... a detail, or a scene that you see in a different light?

That's exactly what happened to me when I was watching the *Joy Luck Club*. I had watched it before, but this time something stuck with me.

It's the scene with An-Mei and her mom.

An-Mei has just come back to her old home, in the throes of divorce. She's outside sitting in the rain, and her mom approaches her. Her mother explains that growing up (the Chinese way), she was taught to swallow her bitterness, value other people's misery, and desire nothing of her own. This is a cycle she has seen in her mother, herself, and now her daughter (despite trying to teach her differently). It came down to not knowing her worth, and she realized it was not too late for her daughter to change.

> *I wanted a man who had buckets and buckets full of patience.*

I had to decide what I was worth... worth as it related to me and what I wanted from a partner. What was it that I wanted in a perfect mate? What was it that I needed from someone to support me?

I knew what I didn't want—I had plenty of wrong dates to make that list a mile long—but when looking at what I wanted from a man, I realized that I had focused on physical characteristics: tall, dark and handsome.

So, I did what most women do best… I made a list. At the very top of the list, I knew for me—a strong, determined, and driven woman—the character trait he needed the most was patience. I wanted a man who had buckets and buckets full of patience, and then more characteristics came to mind—loving, affectionate, wants children, smart, capable, dependable, fun, likes movies… and then somewhere on the list was tall, dark, and handsome… but I didn't lead with those characteristics anymore.

Then I thought about the list but had a sense of releasing it into the world—for Universe, God, Source, whatever you want to call it—to figure it out for me.

Two months later, I met the man who would become my husband.

So, what really happened here?

> *I became crystal clear on what I wanted, deserved, and expected.*

I became crystal clear on what I wanted, deserved, and expected. I fully expected to have this man appear, find me, and pursue me. There's a lovely story behind our courtship, but I'll tell you, he had 95% of what was on my list. Most importantly, he had ALL the top qualities, which in the end was the only thing that mattered.

Three—I Was Empowered

As this seed of value and self-worth was growing, it was nurtured by my hidden strengths… the things that I was "too much of" as a younger child… too demanding, too questioning, too driven… but something else was missing.

Passion.

I did everything I was supposed to do:
College Degree
MBA
Married
Prestigious high-powered corporate job

Pregnant

Didn't I have it all? Education, family, prestige, money... wasn't that enough?

HELL NO!

What I wanted was more impact, a way to help and make a difference in the world. Let's be real, I wanted more money than my corporate job would give me (since what I saw was a lot of sacrifice to achieve wealth, and I wasn't down with that).

> *What I wanted was more impact, a way to help and make a difference in the world.*

So, what was I supposed to do with close to $100,000 in student loan debt? Getting an M.B.A. isn't cheap!

I googled, "What is my passion?"

That didn't really turn up much, and I didn't want to spend any money... because self-discovery is always better on the cheap, right?

It took me a couple years, but two things happened to help me figure out my passion.

The first was fully embracing my strengths.

I've always had a strong personality. Some call it being a leader, others call it being bossy (lol)... and it somehow always seemed to get me into some kind of trouble. I couldn't help it. I've always wanted to lead, inspire and motivate people to do more. I guess I wanted to be for others what I felt had been missing most of my life.

So, after pushing through in my high-paying consulting gig, doing the work that I didn't want to do but doing it so damn well and taking initiative (otherwise known as being arrogant, pushy, and bitchy if you're a woman), opportunity and preparation finally met!

I found a way to make more money for the firm (always a win), created a new standard, and improved processes for the client. How? I was totally ME!

I was the same person I always was, but unapologetically. I pushed, rallied, and empowered. I got shit done and drove some serious results.

I dove head-first into getting promoted, creating a name for myself and grew a positive reputation, so much so that I was awarded their top employee performance award and called out as a "force multiplier" to my complete and utter surprise. (I still had self-worth issues and needed external validation.)

It all started when I decided to stop focusing on what I didn't have and what I was lacking, and to instead focus on leveraging my strengths. I just kept being me until people could see me for the asset I was, and not the liability.

The second was: I got help.

Human beings are social creatures, creating community and support—and for some idiotic reason we are brought up and taught (at least in western culture) that you are supposed to be self-sufficient and succeed on your own. This is complete BS—and a total mind fuck.

If we could solve our problems, then we would do that. We go to doctors, mechanics, accountants to get help. Why on earth don't we do it to figure out what we want to do in life?!

So, I hired a life coach… someone to help me figure it all out. It was the first time I invested in myself. It felt like a "selfish" investment, because I could justify the $80,000 I spent on my MBA as career advancement, but figuring out my passion… wasn't that just silly-ness?

> *My life coach looked at a way forward, instead of rehashing out the past.*

I've been to psychologists, and that was definitely not what I was wanting. I was intrigued because my life coach looked at a way forward, instead of rehashing out the past. That's not to say that psychologists aren't valuable, but my situation called for forward movement!

I needed someone who was able to call my BS (in that tough-love kind of way), help me process all my complex thoughts, and help focus me on what I wanted more of and what I could do to achieve it.

Now this wasn't a magic bullet solution, a cycle I've tended to fall into in the past. You know, the "If you only do this one thing, all your problems will be solved" kind of stuff. I had to do a lot of introspective work, and get in tune with my own voice, a voice I'm not sure I had heard loud and clear since I was young. It was always there, but there were too many other voices that were louder: the "YOU SUCK," "You're not good enough," and "What were you thinking?" voices. Those assholes were always loud and clear.

After a short while—about six months—with some tears, laughter, and breakdowns to get to the breakthroughs—I did my next big investment, a coaching program for $10,000.

At this point, I was married and starting my first IVF journey, so a $10,000 investment wasn't something I could take lightly, but I'm blessed in that my husband has always supported me in growing myself and my business.

Four—I Kept Trying

> *I had new challenges come into play, challenges I never anticipated.*

As I completed my coach training, I had new challenges come into play, challenges I never anticipated. I was a on a whole new path of discovery, one that wasn't laid out by check boxes and corporate achievement. These were unknown metrics and goals I had to identify and achieve… on my own!

So, I started this new journey by identifying more of who I wanted to work with and the kinds of problems I wanted to support solving. I would get such a slap on the wrist right now from my own coaching program for saying "solving problems," because I don't solve problems but help support my client in identifying the solution they want to use to solve their *own* problems.

I giggle now when I think about my first few clients. We worked together trying to identify how I could support them, helping them find their truth and figuring out how to take action to get their desired results.

I giggle because I realize that not much has changed in how I show up for my clients—I'm still full of love, action, and willingness to cheer them past their finish line. But my goodness, the evolution from Cat 2013 to Cat 2018? Five years isn't a long time, but my business has seen three lives since then.

I coached hundreds of kinds of clients in a variety of industries, careers, and business stages. What I found through all this was that I could get the best results for people who had been where I was. #SHOCKER!

> *We are our clients. We are a version of them, be it one day ago, or ten years ago.*

You've likely heard it before… but *we* are our clients. We are a version of them, be it one day ago, or ten years ago. We have walked their path, and we as coaches and consultants can show them how to avoid the pitfalls and get them better and faster results!

Nelson Mandela says, "You never fail, you either learn or succeed," and I can apply this philosophy to all aspects of my past and future.

Five—I Got Naked

Yes—I kept spending money. Once I realized how a business of my own could set me free, I knew I had to learn more.

So, I invested another $16,000 in two years of a mastermind and $10,000 in a done-for-you marketing expert.

Here's what I learned…

First, you can *learn* all you want, but unless you *act*, you aren't going to get results.

Second, NEVER, and I mean NEVER give up your power and believe that someone else can fix all your "problems" for you without your active participation. Yeah, I fell for the magic bullet again. But, I learned a valuable lesson. I learned that I am the driver, pusher, creator, and the ultimate responsible party for my business.

I must understand foundational concepts to build the empire I want, and the reason I must know and appreciate the foundational pieces is that those are the things that *you* are building upon, too.

> *I am the driver, pusher, creator, and the ultimate responsible party for my business.*

So, if you don't master the basic skills, knowing your ideal client, relationship marketing, networking, and speaking (be it Facebook live, teaching moments, or 300+ attendee conferences), your business will not succeed to the level you want.

Why?

Because you have to know and be inside your ideal client's head, so you can speak their language, attract them, communicate the benefits of working with you, and convert them into clients!

Now…back to getting naked.

I realized that part of me was still being hidden by a corporate façade, holding me back from really being out there and differentiating myself from all the other coaches out there, because there are so many!

I went all out and hired a brand specialist, and we came up with Action Incubator. I'll admit we went a little too far with some of the pics, but don't worry, those aren't on the website.

I have always loved attention! I had to go all-out to an extreme, to come to a place where I felt that I was finally being seen for who I was, unapologetically.

Finally pulling all my passions into one place—movies, action, strategy, coaching, consulting—put me in such a powerful place! I felt unstoppable and empowered to do more than ever before, because I felt real, different, and inexcusably out there for the world to see.

EMPIRE BUILDER

CAT STANCIK

There's no such thing as a Mission Impossible to Cat Stancik, who is known for her tough love approach that gets clients into focused action so that they can get out of overwhelm and create big results with significantly less effort! She works with high achieving entrepreneurs who want to stop focusing on the glorified 6 and 7 figure marks, and finally enjoy a profitable, balanced business. Cat does this by leveraging her proprietary system, to simplify, strategize and systematize to an entirely new level.

Cat is the founder of Action Incubator™, a sought-after speaker, and Bestselling Author of *7 Principles for a More Productive and Fulfilling Life*. As a self-proclaimed "Education Junkie" who genuinely cares about honing her coaching skills to get her clients better and bigger results, getting an MBA wasn't enough for Cat Stancik. She's also certified by The Coaches Training Institute, the

Project Management Institute, and the Leadership Circle Profile 360 Assessment. She is also a long-time member of the International Coaching Federation, where she holds her ACC. She lives in Maryland with her two daughters and her adoring husband, who showers her with chocolate and massages (if he knows what's good for him).

To access Cat's gift, go to empirebuildersgift.com/bonus.

LINDA POTEET

WHEN YOUR GUT AND DECISIONS LEAD YOU HOME

One of the hardest things to do in business is to listen to your gut. There is a vast amount of advice out there, and often we want to dive in and create cash flow. We want the fast track and believe that the knowledge and skills for a successful business are somewhere outside of us. We see influential leaders and competitors with incredible businesses and wonder if we will ever succeed as entrepreneurs.

That belief is not your fault because what most gurus are not telling you is this: Your entrepreneurial journey will take bends and twists until you stop and listen to your gut and get clear on what you are meant to do in the world.

> *Stop and listen to your gut and get clear on what you are meant to do in the world.*

My business journey is a winding path, filled with self-doubt and decisions that left me questioning what I was thinking, intertwined with moments of great celebration.

In venturing the entrepreneurial path, I founded three companies which allowed me to really learn what works and what doesn't, through the school of hard knocks.

EMPIRE BUILDERS

But for now, let's head back to where my vision for what I would do in life began. I grew up on a farm with a beautiful view in the hills of Oregon. I would spend my summers outside, and in the winter, I would devour every magazine I could get my mom to buy for me. I loved magazines, the stories, the images, and the exotic locations I could imagine visiting.

> *I lived a carefree, luscious, adventurous life in the California wine country.*

When I was about fourteen, our family started traveling to different places all over the world. Whenever we visited places like Sonoma, California, Greece, or Italy, I felt at home. I think in a way it was the combination of "farm" that I found in the gorgeous vineyards, lemon and olive groves, and the beautiful people and buildings that I remembered from my magazines, that felt amazing.

After I graduated with a degree in communications and mass media, I moved to Sonoma and started my career at a public relations firm. I lived a carefree, luscious, adventurous life in the California wine country. I spent my days working on media campaigns and my nights socializing with friends over a scrumptious dinner and a glass of wine, before a sunset walk through the vineyards.

Flash forward a decade and you would find me a single mom, in debt, overweight, trying to build a business, while working a full-time job, recovering from a year of battling cancer, and doing work that left me feeling empty. You see, somewhere along the way, I left PR and went into Human Resources. And, I left the places that felt so good to me to live. I stopped following my heart and listened to the "should" of other people.

I describe my life at that point as joyless and stuck, and yet, when I thought about wanting more for my life, I often felt guilty because as I looked around, my blessings were many. Guilt was something I dealt with many times in my life. I made choices but I was worried about what others said I should do or believed I should do. I made decisions by over-thinking everything and complicating my life.

After living like that for many years, I was on a trip to Sonoma when an idea sparked in my mind to design a great travel handbag that was functional and beautiful. That is how Juxees, my handbag company, was born.

If you are a product-based business owner, you know that it can be an extremely expensive endeavor. I purchased leather from Brazil, manufactured in China and Los Angeles, shipped, and then shipped again to customers, attended trade shows and "Market." I created handbag sample after handbag sample, to make sure it was just right before manufacturing. While I loved the design aspect, the rest was EXPENSIVE! I finally concluded that unless I manufactured in enormous quantities, I would never surpass the break-even point. I learned that having a business plan does not always result into the predicted profit.

In 2014, I closed my handbag company. Did it fail? No, it provided me with tremendous learning opportunities. Taking the things that you struggle with in a business and turning them into a lesson for what to do next time is the key to any business success. There were numerous times in my handbag business that I did not listen to my own intuition, especially when it came to marketing. I even tried setting it up as a multi-level marketing company (MLM) and I personally don't even like the MLM business model. It has extreme regulations and expenses. That decision left me with $90,000 of debt before I closed the business.

> *Having a business plan does not always result into the predicted profit.*

When I closed Juxees, I was heartbroken and disappointed in myself. I was frustrated and almost gave up on my business dreams.

But then I traveled again, this time to Sorrento, Italy. I was standing on a cliff overlooking the Mediterranean when a building caught my eye. It was worn down and the paint was chipping, but if you looked closely enough, you could see its beauty. As I stood there looking at that building, tears began to stream down my face, because what I saw in that building was myself.

I had again given up on the life I had dreamed about. I was just existing and not truly living my dreams. After that trip to Italy and my decision to jump back into business, I took the PLUNGE! This time I created a life coaching business, but I was unfulfilled, and I was *still* not working in my zone of genius.

My whole life I had yearned to be around the media. So, in working with a business coach, I made the decision to rebrand as "Yellow Fish," a publicity and media marketing company. I was determined to go back to what I know best and to do a service and information-based business where the overhead is less costly. This business model works with much more ease for me. I love media coaching and publicity. If I can get someone placed in a top-tier magazine, it is a great day!

> *There is extreme power in building credibility, clout, and influence via media.*

This time, I built my business through one of the best kept secrets in the industry—free publicity. There is extreme power in building credibility, clout, and influence via media.

There are five reasons getting booked, featured, or quoted in the media is important to your business.

Getting featured in the media helps you stand out in front of potential customers who need what you're selling. Even small media appearances can lead to significant sales increase.

Getting featured in the media positions you as an expert with ideas that ought to be seen, heard, and shared.

If sales feel "icky" to you, getting featured in the media is an opportunity for you to "sell" gracefully without having to sell aggressively.

Getting in the media helps you build relationships by "giving away" some of your expertise.

Media opportunities, if done correctly, open more doors.

When I launched, I sent out my first press release and did radio interviews for my book, *Celebrate Your Deliciousness*. This book was born out of inspiration that came to me when I was out for a run one day. The press for this book was crazy! Suddenly, I was on CBS, NBC, I Heart Radio, and more as my book went to #3 on the Amazon bestseller list.

> *Media opportunities, if done correctly, open more doors.*

Today, I've received over 700 media mentions in places like I Heart Radio, Spotlight Magazine, CBS, NBC, ABC, BingeTV, RokuTV, FOX, The CW, The Traveler… Those appearances have transformed into my own WebTV show that will be released soon on Roku, a new book deal, $70,000 in speaking revenue, and probably most of my clients, because up until now, I have never done paid advertising. And, I've never paid a dime for media coverage.

In the eight months after that first press release, I paid off that $90,000 of debt!

The Decision

For me, there have been key decision points all along my business journey. All seem to happen when I travel, but that's a whole different chapter. For now, let's stick with the decision.

- Life often comes down to one or two key decisions that can change your life, defining moments that you will remember your entire life, where you draw a line in the sand, and commit to your destiny.
- One of my decisions was to focus on publicity and media, the thing that I knew best and was in my zone of genius.

- I realized that no decision is a "bad" decision; instead, it is an opportunity to grow.
- Decisions from our heart and intuition take us further than head space decisions.

> *Take some time to get out and enjoy the beauty around you and do something new.*

In business, lessons constantly appear. What I've learned is that profiting in business comes down to three things: your key decisions, listening to your inner quiet voice, and working in an area that is your true gift. Your inner voice and gifts will guide you to your greatest desires and the place where you can make the greatest impact and income.

Today, not only do I have my publicity and marketing agency that I hope to sell in 3-5 years, but I have just started my third business, Olivelimone, a lifestyle company that includes our farm, tasting room, product line, magazine, and we hope to expand one day into commercial properties with Lemon Grove Suites. This is a combination of product-based and information-based model. Through all my lessons in business, I am excited to bring this company—my passion project—to life in a much more informed way. Olivelimone all came from listening to what my soul wanted and trusting my gut enough to say, YES!

One of the things that I have learned along the way, is that none of my decisions were "bad" per se, each of my business adventures had a purpose. Each adventure helped hone a different skill set. And, all led me back to my dream and where I feel most at home, in the Olive Groves.

As we close this chapter, I hope you will take some time to get out and enjoy the beauty around you and do something new. In the quiet moments is when our greatest inspiration and key decisions are realized.

Cheers to you and your beautiful entrepreneurial journey. I'd like to leave you with this quote:

"Always trust your gut, it knows what your head hasn't figured out yet."

—Anonymous

EMPIRE BUILDER

LINDA POTEET

Linda Poteet is a publicity and authority marketing specialist for small business owners and the founder of Yellow Fish Fortunes. As an international speaker, best-selling author and a business coach, Linda believes the way you show up in the world and your expertise is your biggest asset. She inspires entrepreneurs from around the globe to tap into their unique gifts, show up and be visible, take consistent action and have the systems in place to grow a profitable business.

Armed with a degree in Mass Communications and Media and a Masters in Leadership, Linda has over the past twenty-five years helped large and small businesses in the areas of public relations, advertising, communication, executive coaching, leadership training and owned three companies.

To access Linda's gift, go to empirebuildersgift.com/bonus.

JEN LEVITZ

THE CASTLE

Since 2002, I've worked with hundreds of clients and helped them translate their ideas into a business with a solid structure that allows them to sustainably grow and scale, while signaling to the world they are ready to soar.

While the majority of the time we lean on my experience working with various marketing and automation technology systems to reach our desired goals, business success still relies on people. I've found it is important to understand the optimal frame of mind needed to achieve your outcome.

As I see it, choosing to become the owner of a new business is VERY similar to buying a castle.

Both require you to dream big and see things as they will be in the future while you make do with what's available right now.

> *Become the owner of a new business is VERY similar to buying a castle.*

Both could be considered "high-risk" by the family and friends closest to you.

Most likely, both will need a steady cash flow to keep things running smoothly.

But when you feel called to own either, it's hard to be dissuaded from taking the leap.

If you are anything like me, you probably picked up this book to learn a few ways to set yourself up for success. You see, for me, the more information I gather, the safer a "risky" venture becomes.

> *The more information I gather, the safer a "risky" venture becomes.*

When you start out in business, it's as if you have bought an empty castle. It doesn't come with servants (or house elves), so everything that needs to be done to make the castle liveable really needs to be handled by YOU.

This is especially true if you are starting up on a shoestring budget. You may be able to bring in some help for bigger things, but generally you're going to be the one running up and down the stairs as you juggle being IN your business with clients and working ON your business to bring in more clients and move the business forward.

Let's apply this idea of a castle to YOUR business.

First, start with the assumption that YOUR castle really has four areas or levels to it: The Towers, the Private Areas (i.e., the bedrooms and private studies on the upper floors), the Main Floor (i.e., the public areas of the castle, including the library, ballroom, and sitting rooms), and Downstairs (i.e., the kitchen and servant's areas.)

Each of these areas serves its own purpose and the mentality needed to allow each to function optimally is also different.

Now remember, when you are new and don't (yet) have the funds to bring in a staff to help, managing and operating each of these areas falls to you, so let's explore each level so you can have a better sense of how things function.

The Towers

This area is home to the Visionary, the CEO of your business. From here, you look out the window and see the entirety of your "Enchanted Empire." It supports all that you want to do *in, with,* and *for* your business.

This is where you nurture your BIG DREAMS to become the ideas that you put into action. Up here, you and your thoughts reside together in a space of your own. It's likely this area of the castle is what inspired you to start a business in the first place.

Unfortunately, because there are so many stairs between the other parts of the house and the Towers, in the early years it's likely this area won't see regular use. However, I highly recommend that you schedule a few days per year to fully embody your CEO vibe. That will keep you connected and on track with your overall future vision.

The Private Areas

As we head down from the towers, we end up in the domain of the Strategist. Here, focus splits a bit as we have two different types of people to serve.

First, you have your "honored guests," your paying clients. It's at this level that you help your clients meet their goals. It doesn't matter if they purchase done-for-you, done-with-you, or a do-it-yourself product or program, all client work happens here (behind closed doors).

> *Schedule a few days per year to fully embody your CEO vibe.*

This is also where you work on your own business, as the resident of the castle. Your thoughts and ideas from the towers are turned into projects that can be planned and actioned on in the levels below.

In the Private Areas of your castle, you are grounded in the reality of how things are, while still focusing on your intended or promised outcome.

If your business has a business integrator, coach, or an executive team, they are likely operating in this mental place most of the time, as they are focused on delivery and fulfillment.

The Main Floor

If in the Private Areas you *earn* your money, it's on the Main Floor where you *make* your money.

The Main Floor of the castle, with its public spaces, is the Planner's domain. It's the prospect and potential client-facing side of your business. Mentally, it's managing the NOW while trying to balance that with the near(ish) future, generally about a month at a time. It's where the strategy turns into an actual and tactical plan.

In the digital landscape, the title Online Business Manager (OBM) generally takes on the Butler role. Just like a Butler, an OBM is attuned to the pulse of the business. They make sure that things are getting done "Downstairs" while making sure that the clients in the upper levels are being looked after, along with ensuring that the prospects and leads on this level are having a good experience.

> *Look to Virtual Assistants who have experience in the tasks you want to complete.*

While it's tempting to hire an OBM as quickly as possible, keep in mind that their role is really one of management. They help keep your "Downstairs" team (and you) moving forward on the projects created at the Strategist level.

Instead of jumping in and hiring an OBM when you are just starting out, I recommend looking to Virtual Assistant Agencies who have experience in the tasks you want to complete. Yes, you will likely be paying more per hour; however, they will also manage the project and execute the tasks more efficiently.

Additionally, there are a lot of low-cost technology options available to help with nurturing (and entertaining) the guests in your public spaces. Many of these tools require you to put in some effort to set them up, then will need little attention to keep them working. For instance, your website, besides updating your copy every once in a while, really only needs you to add blog content weekly. Or your Email Marketing System… once you have set up a few auto-responders, it really only needs you to write and send your newsletter.

So really, this level is more about the mental energy of nurturing, whether it's to nurture your potential clients or having your "Butler" nurture your team of technicians or the technology.

Downstairs

The Downstairs area is the home of the Technician and it's the primary space where things get done. In your business, this is where much of the "behind the scenes" magic happens to keep the business running on a day-to-day basis. The thought process on this level is limited in vision.

> *As a business owner, Downstairs is often the most difficult area to navigate.*

At the most basic level, when you are in technician mode, you are head-down in the work of the moment and are oblivious to everything else around you. You're focused on the NOW with, maybe, a peek to a few days from now.

Most virtual team members, especially the ones on the lower end of the pay scale, tend to be excellent "Technicians." They complete the detailed tasks to which they are assigned. (This is similar to what a general house maid and kitchen staff would do.)

As a business owner, Downstairs is often the most difficult area to navigate. Because you need to make the rest of the household "go," it is likely there are skills that you NEED to hire out. Either you don't possess those skills OR (worse yet) you *can* do it, but they will keep you from doing the things that you, and you alone MUST do.

Word of advice here: if you can do the task yourself, then hiring it out to a lower-cost Virtual Assistant (VA) is a great idea, because you will already know all they need to do to complete the task. (Because remember, YOU are managing them.) If you don't already know the task, be willing to invest more money to have the project managed FOR you. If your VA can't give you a detailed scope of work for that task, they may not be the right person to *do* and *manage* the task.

Navigating the Castle

Now that you've taken the tour, you may be wondering how to use this information to your best advantage.

First, I recommend that you PLAN to spend most of your time on the main floor. This will allow you to serve clients one level up and get things done one level down. Be cautious, however, to not schedule yourself in such a way that you need to shift directly from "Doing" to "Serving" or vice-versa. When possible, give yourself space on the main floor, as a buffer, between those tasks so as not to burn yourself out, because shifting from Downstairs to the Private Spaces takes a lot more energy.

> *PLAN to spend most of your time on the main floor.*

You'll also want to schedule time to visit the towers a couple of times a year to help keep you excited about your business. Pair that with focused time to work on creating the strategic plan to action the higher-level ideas for your business. For instance, if you go to an event where you are likely to get new ideas, plan on extending your trip so you can do some planning before you slip back into "normal" life.

Now that I've shared these four levels… do you agree that owning a business is like owning a castle?

Over the past 15+ years, my business has evolved and the types of services I offer and the clients I work with have too. Where I really started out in the role of the technician, being the "doer" in many six- and seven-figure businesses, I quickly shifted to more of that "butler" role where I needed to understand the strategies so that I could translate those needs to others, so *they* could get the job done.

Nowadays, though, I spend most of my time in the "Private Areas," helping business owners choose the best business models and strategies to bring their big business ideas to life, along with creating the tactical plan to make it all happen. With a plan in hand, my clients feel empowered to delegate tasks, knowing that by doing so it keeps everyone moving forward, faster.

EMPIRE BUILDER

JEN LEVITZ

Jen Levitz is a Business Wizard & Coach as well as the Head Mistress of SpellbindingBusinessSchool.com

Jen once lived the life of a Business Muggle, struggling to make ends meet, at times feeling powerless, and wishing she could just take a quick broomstick ride to success.

Marketing felt complicated.

She avoided it at all costs—helping everyone but herself.

Until one day Jen discovered the magical blend that would change her life forever... A dash of proven Business Models, a pinch of Signature Systems, a sprinkle of the simplest Marketing, and a healthy dose of just the right Mindset.

Her business began boiling over with clients.

Today, Jen teaches entrepreneurs how to brew their own special profit potions too!

To access Jen's gift, go to empirebuildersgift.com/bonus.

DEE MOULTRIE

PROFIT IS YOUR #1 GOAL

My business, First Class to Profit, helps entrepreneurs learn how to run profitable businesses. We take a "profit-first" approach, ensuring that the business owner remains profitable from the first day. We are on a mission to eradicate entrepreneurial poverty.

Like many of the authors in this book, I have the benefit of perspective to look back on the tough times of my life. I can recall several occasions when I relied completely on grace and grit, and there were other times where I relied on grace and *eventually* my grit kicked in. I'll share three experiences that are always top of mind...

I made a commitment over nineteen years ago to the love of my life who gave me three of my greatest blessings, my sons. Yes, I am a mother of three sons, no daughters, and before you ask, yes, this is it.

> *I relied on grace and eventually my grit kicked in.*

"I, De'Lona Moultrie will not be a mother of a daughter in this lifetime... I, De'Lona Moultrie have completed *my child-bearing-ness and therefore no girl, I will instead steal a few girls in my family and get my fix."* :)

Although it's not one of my top reflections of tough times, I think it goes without saying that being married for nineteen years and a mother to all sons has required a great deal of grace and grit. This fact alone should credit me with some kind of bona-fide certification in both. All jokes aside, being a wife and mother has been the hardest work of my life, BUT I can say it has also been the most rewarding. I am thankful that I didn't quit, and I don't know where I would be without grace and grit.

Before I got married, I was hit by a car while standing INSIDE a building, and rushed to the emergency room. I have every reason to believe it was supposed to be my last day on earth, yet I LIVED to tell the story.

My oldest son was told at the age of seven that he would not be able to walk, let alone run, yet this year he ended his football season as one of the leading running backs in central Ohio. My second son is a leading receiver, and my third son kicked off his high school career with a great start on JV.

> *The real estate bug hit us, and hasn't ever let go.*

My husband and I almost lost everything during the 2008-2009 market crash. I was IN the financial industry during those years. I ran a financial consulting business and everything we owned was tied to the financial sector, including our real estate portfolio valued at over a million at the time.

My husband and I were fortunate enough to buy my grandmother's home at a steep discount in 1998. I wanted to keep that home in the family, and apparently so did my grandmother, so she helped us greatly with the price. That generosity led to the purchase of our dream home a few years later. The real estate bug hit us, and hasn't ever let go, even after the real estate crash.

The recession hit us hard, though. Overnight, our income dropped. Herm temporarily lost his job, and my income was completely gone. During this time, it seemed like we were barely hanging on; that ended with me eventually taking an unplanned sabbatical.

The sabbatical lasted a little over three years, and, with the exception of not having the cash flow that we were used to, I have no regrets. But, when the bills started changing color (pink and red!), we eventually filed Chapter 13, a restructuring of our debt. Miraculously, two of the banks to which we owed money forgave the remainder of the mortgages, leaving us owning them free and clear, which was the catalyst to helping us get our finances back on track.

> *I could have quit, and some days I certainly felt like it.*

I could have quit, and some days I certainly felt like it. I could have balled up in my bed for the rest of my life. Some days I did that too, but something made me get up…

…GRACE AND GRIT!

And my two passions: family and business.

Today, as a darn proud wife and momma, I run a high-level business mentorship program for a select number of entrepreneurs. We focus on creating profits in our businesses.

Being a wife is what makes me happy. Being Mom is what makes me happy. Entrepreneurship is what makes me happy. Helping entrepreneurs run profitable businesses with grace and grit makes me happy. And that's why I do what I do.

I am a firm believer that grace, that unmerited, undeserved favor, can take you places that hustling simply can't. So I encourage you to engage grace in every aspect of your life and business.

Always remember, grit is the unique quality that makes you willing and ready to commit yourself to your long-term goals and pursue them despite any adversity that you may face. It is defined as having a firm character and an indomitable spirit.

What About You?

Every year in the United States, more than 627,000 new businesses open, according to estimates from the Small Business Administration, the SBA. That's more than half a million people leaving their 9 to 5 job to set out on their own. Unfortunately, not everyone is cut out to be a small business owner, as evident by the nearly 595,000 businesses that *close* every year. To those companies that get off the ground and keep running, only 51 percent remain in business for more than five years.

> *Do you have a life plan?*

With such disheartening numbers, you may be wondering if you should venture out on your own and start a business, and whether you'll succeed as an entrepreneur.

My answer is emphatically, YES! The rewards of entrepreneurship are invaluable! But, to have success in any endeavor, especially entrepreneurship, you will need to have both grace and grit.

By learning these concepts, you can start to work toward incorporating these practices into your own life and entrepreneurial journey and find your personal success. Here are some powerful shifts I've learned in my journey that I hope will be a blessing to you:

Shift 1: Develop Your Prosperity Plan

Business plans and marketing plans may be great, but do you have a *life* plan? Our businesses should be serving our lives, but very few entrepreneurs are able to make that happen. Before we start talking about revenue and marketing goals, we need to understand what we want in our lives. Build a business that supports your life, not the other way around.

Shift 2: Profit First

We have the formula mixed up. Profit is typically thought of as revenue less expenses, and then the amount left over is profit. Instead, take your profit first, directly from your revenue, and then pay everything else. There is a huge difference between profit and revenue; they're not the same, and most people focus almost completely on revenue.

Shift 3: Don't Fly Solo in Your Business

You will find tremendous power in mentorship and coaching. You don't have to make your own mistakes. When you have a mentor, you can learn from the mentor's mistakes and avoid common pitfalls. Great coaches teach that you should never hold on to your past failures or mistakes. They share their history as a means of valuable training, so you don't make the same mistakes in the future.

Don't Stress Over Things You Can't Control

> *There is no point in wasting your time on things you can't control.*

There is no point in wasting your time on things you can't control. There will be times in your life that you won't have any control over what is happening. When this happens, you need to remember not to give the obstacles any importance and do what you plan to do anyway. If you want to gain the success you desire, you must let go of the things you can't control. It's what all people who have engaged grace and grit do.

Be Conscious of Your Blessings

People who possess grit aren't just dedicated to their mission and aren't only working on strengthening their minds; they are also cognizant of all the blessings that have been bestowed upon them and are conscious of them. They know how truly blessed they are and don't take any of it for granted. This is how they improve their lives continually. This helps them find and invite better opportunities and experiences into their lives.

> *There is no point in wasting your time on things you can't control.*

This is exactly what you will need to do if you want to become successful. You need to spend time every night thinking about everything you are blessed with and stop worrying about the things that you don't have. This will help you to feel better about yourself and encourage you to strive for even better things.

Celebrate the Success of Those Around You

Everyone becomes happy when they achieve success. However, to be genuine you need to celebrate the victories of your peers and competitors. This will help you to achieve the mental strength you need to be successful in your ventures. Genuine people don't frown when their competitors achieve success. Instead, they applaud their success and hard work. Praising successful people brings them closer to you, and when you surround yourself with successful people, you learn new and amazing things to help you improve your life.

Where I'm Going…

I look forward to continuing my year-long mastermind program for entrepreneurs, where I train new and established business owners to build and scale profitably. In addition, I have been teaching real estate investing and was offered the opportunity to open a branch office of a financing company, called First Class Financial. I still do administrative consulting with a focus on operations and recently signed on a new client, an accountant who wants to outsource some of her client work and go into coaching.

Most of all, I enjoy teaching entrepreneurs how to become profitable. If I had only two words to say to you, they would be "Profit first!"

EMPIRE BUILDER

DE'LONA "DEE" MOULTRIE

Author of the book, *Resilience Factor*, and with over 25 years experience in the consulting field, De'Lona "Dee" Moultrie founded First Class to Profit to help entrepreneurs create profitable businesses while working less.

Dee began as an Independent Financial Consultant supporting families with personal finances, insurance planning, debt elimination, and credit restoration. She co-owned a very successful Real Estate Investment company with her husband, as well as a family business selling personalized books for children.

Dee has a knack for systematizing business operations so that they run efficiently, allowing entrepreneurs to get more done in less time. If you want your business to run more organized with smoother and more profitable operations, Dee is the expert you need to talk to!

To access Dee's gift, go to empirebuildersgift.com/bonus.

Amanda Goldman-Petri

Empire Building Like a Nerd

"What's possible has been done; what's impossible must be done."

—Anonymous

I am the founder of Market Like a Nerd™, where I work with coaches, teaching them how to work smarter, not harder by increasing their prices and leveraging high ticket offers, all while traveling the world on amazing, once-in-a-lifetime retreats.

Life is amazing now, but it hasn't always been that way. In fact, it was far from it. I was born in Baltimore, Maryland, also known as Body More, Murderland. Are you familiar with the television show, *The Wire*? Well, that's where I grew up. We didn't live in a great part of the city, either.

In addition to that, my family is crazy psycho-nuts. I'm talking schizophrenics, kleptomaniacs, felons, drunks, rapists, and every other bag of crazy you can think of.

> *Life is amazing now, but it hasn't always been that way.*

My dad's side of the family wasn't any better. My biological father was a drug addict who spent time in and out of jail. I distinctly remember a time when we were going to the Butterfly

Gardens in Maryland. I looked over and saw a homeless man on a bus stop bench. Looking closer, I realized it was my father. I was mortified. Another time, I saw my dad on the subway and he didn't even recognize me. He only spoke to me because he thought I looked like my aunt. A few years later, he called me from jail to tell me I was going to be a big sister. Apparently, after getting a prostitute pregnant, he thought we'd be a family again.

> *I realized that if I had died in that accident, I wouldn't have lived a good life.*

My older brother and I were physically abused by our stepfather. Finally, my mom hit a breaking point and was done with men. She decided to be with a woman and left my stepfather. Later, I testified against my stepfather in a custody hearing, and he threatened to kill me.

Right about that time, I was involved in a major accident. On June 17, 2008, an 80-year-old man, speeding at 50 miles per hour in his minivan, hit me as I was walking across the street. My leg collapsed into the grill and then gravity pulled my body upwards, my head shattering the windshield. He slammed on his brakes and I flew into the intersection, landing one fortunate foot away from being crushed by a passing 18-wheeler.

I was in shock trauma for a week, then gradually started physical therapy. My biggest question was whether I would go to college in the fall. I had received congressional nominations to the Naval Academy, the Merchant Marine Academy, and West Point, as well as a full-ride scholarship to the Johns Hopkins University. Ultimately, I decided to take the challenge and went to Johns Hopkins the year after the accident. After realizing that if I had died in that accident, I wouldn't have lived a good life, I decided to reevaluate what I wanted to do.

I was ready to find out who I was, but life wasn't finished with me yet. In November of my freshman year, I found out I was pregnant. The only thing was… I didn't even remember conceiving. Apparently it happened when I was bed-ridden from the car accident. I decided to keep the baby and press on.

Turning Points

I think all the time about why I didn't go down a different path. I could have easily made different decisions that would have changed everything. Thinking back on it, my mom was my saving grace. She nurtured me and my resilience from a very young age.

One clear turning point stands out in my mind. It was after I learned I was pregnant. My mom met me at school and we sat together on a marble bench in the quad. That was when she told me she intended to leave my stepfather, except she was worried about money. I told her that if that was all she was worried about, I'd work as many jobs as I had to, to support her, my brothers, my baby, and me, if only she would help me care for my baby. We decided we'd make it work and could get through it if we supported each other. That year, I lived between Mom's house, my dorm, and my future husband Jason's house.

In college, one of the three jobs I had to help Mom pay the mortgage was as a telemarketer. I was quite good at it. Within three or four months, I had generated between $50,000 and $60,000 in donations for Johns Hopkins. I was the number two caller in the entire call room with one of the lists that should have been the worst-performing. At the time, I didn't realize I was learning a skill. I looked at it as a job, but I was really learning about sales.

> *I could have easily made different decisions that would have changed everything.*

I am a very multi-passionate person and growing up I wanted to do a million things. At Johns Hopkins, I started my degree studying medicine. I started as neuroscience major and wanted to be a neurosurgeon. Growing up as I did, I looked at professions that would change my life, like medicine or law, but as much as I like science, it's not really my passion. My neuroscience major soon turned into cellular and molecular biology, then the natural sciences. If you'll notice, these are the sciences on decreasing levels of difficulty. Going to Johns Hopkins is tough; it's like you're learning an entire semester in one day. Pretty soon, I started taking classes based on interest. By the time I was done, I had earned triple majors in creative writing, the Russian language, and East Asian studies. In the same time it takes people to earn one, I had earned three. I had to try everything.

> *I thought life was supposed to be hard.*

After I graduated, I decided to go to grad school at an easier school. I took an easy major studying writing to bide time until I decided what I wanted to do. I still needed to make money, so I took a job as a social media marketing intern at minimum wage. It introduced me to a whole new world. This is where I met Mara Glazer, Christine Gallagher, Michelle PW, and other women entrepreneurs. They were making lots of money, working from home, really happy, and spending time with their family. I didn't realize this kind of life was a possibility. I thought life was supposed to be hard. Realizing that was not the case, I decided I wanted that dream life for myself and my family too.

Around this time, I married Jason. Jason had a completely different upbringing than mine: he is upper class, well off, and stable, with no drama or scandals. His family is made up of doctors, lawyers, and fortune 500 company owners. They're normal. They come together for reunions and actually *want* to see each other. It's such a different life. At first, I was uncomfortable with it. It wasn't normal to me to have no drama and I didn't trust it. It was almost like I was trying to push it away. I thought it was all a disguise and that under it all, he'd be as broken as I was.

When I married Jason and while I was working with amazing women entrepreneurs, it was like the universe was telling me things could be better. I didn't have to be the way my family was. I decided to listen to the universe.

The Partnership

After six months as Mara Glazer's social media marketing intern, I quit graduate school, I quit all of my jobs, and I started my own business. I found a website company to create the website for this new business and when they discovered my background in social media, we decided to trade services. The deal was that if the company would build my website, I'd do their social media. We ended up hitting it off. They brought me into their web design company and taught me everything. I took all my organization skills and saw their gaps and areas for improvement in their systems and automation. I ended up systematizing their entire business model so they'd be ok when I left to start my own virtual assistant and web design agency. To grow my business, I engaged in Facebook groups, where people would ask me to help with their SEO, graphic design, and web support.

I kept in touch with Mara and we met one October, on her 28th birthday. I flew in and went to a club downtown to meet her for drinks. I made some offhand comment about business being ok but how I would like to make more money. I told her I wanted to make $100,000 per year by the

> *I ended up systematizing their entire business model.*

time I was 28. Mara told me I could do it sooner than that and make much more than that, so I joined Mara's coaching program, which was $12,000 plus money for traveling. I borrowed money from Jason to make it happen. Within four months, I had my first $10,000 month. I was 22. I converted almost all of Mara's mastermind members into virtual assistant clients, including Mara. Mara opened up a Facebook ads agency with some big names in the industry, and hired me to support her clients with Facebook ads. One of our clients spent just $700 in ads and made over $100,000 in sales.

Then, things started to get tricky. Mara was running a done-for-you agency, and I was running a done-for-you agency. Mara became worried about people finding out I was the one doing the work. Our non-compete, non-disclosure discussion became a partnership and we created The Best Damn Biz Team when I was 23. We were successful; in four months, we made over $150,000 in sales. Another month, we had 100 new copywriting clients come in. Despite our success, it felt like more work than it needed to be. I wanted to create systems, automation, and scaling, but my vision and approach didn't align with Mara's.

At that point, I was pregnant with my second son Alex. While I was in labor, Mara called with an emergency. It was then that I realized my life was out of balance. Ultimately, Mara and I dissolved our partnership.

New Beginnings

> *Despite our success, it felt like more work than it needed to be.*

Then I started my coaching business, as Goldman-Petri Coaching, which felt like a temporary brand even at the time. I had just had a child, closed a business down, and was starting a new one. This didn't translate into much in savings. We had debt collectors calling us all the time. I needed to make money right away but not fall into the same trap as before. I did a 30-day push to get one-on-one clients. Now that I had enough money to live on, it was time to focus on the long run.

I got really stubborn. If I didn't like doing something, I was not going to do it anymore. I fully embraced my introverted self. If it required any extroverted tendencies, I didn't do it. My business became my safe place. It allowed me to be me as I embodied who I am and loved myself. Within 90 days, I made $120,000 my way. It finally felt easy.

Once I saw it was working, I decided to go all-out with it. That's when Market Like a Nerd was born. I wanted everything to feel aligned, so I embraced my quirky, weird, dorky, funny side. While I was waiting for my website and branding to be finished, I decided to step into the spotlight. Working with someone as famous as Mara Glazer, I always felt I was living in someone else's shadow. I decided it was time for that to change. I started to hang out with millionaires and I found that level of success is not special. It's normal to work part-time, make millions, and have your dream life. Actually, it's not just possible, it's *normal*. I shifted my mindset and no longer thought I'd have to burn myself out to make more money. I wanted to make more and still be happy. I took lessons from these millionaires, got 50 podcast interviews in 60 days, appeared in *Forbes*, Fast Company, and launched another program my way. I made $562,000 in four months.

> *I started to hang out with millionaires and I found that level of success is not special.*

Entrepreneurship Has Its Challenges

After the $562,000 launch, about six months into delivering those services, I started to have heart issues. My heart was racing at 117 beats per minute, sitting down, and I had palpitations. It triggered my PTSD from the accident and I was very anxious. I went to doctor after doctor and did test after test. It was challenging because it showed there is always more opportunity to make a business more scalable and sustainable. I started to wonder: what happens if I'm in the hospital, or if I die? What's my disaster plan?

I realized being an entrepreneur had taken a toll on my health. Before the accident, I had always been healthy. I had been captain of my soccer team all four years of high school and had a great six pack. After the accident and having my child, my health started to decline. My wrists hurt, my neck hurt, I had a lump on the back of my neck, and my heart was not as healthy as it should have been. I realized how much being entrepreneur can affect your health. So, I went on a health crusade to find out what was wrong with my heart. It turns out I had an inflammation called pericarditis, and that just two weeks of maxing out on ibuprofen would cure it. I went back to the gym, got a personal trainer, and now I work out every day. I am confident in my body finally, again. I make my health a part of everyday life and have implemented high performance habits.

> *I realized how much being entrepreneur can affect your health.*

The second thing I changed was to implement disaster planning. I brought on a business partner, Jodi Sodini. The partnership is strategic but it's also part of our disaster plan. If anything happens to me, she can carry on my legacy.

What I Learned

My very first epiphany was that making money working from home was even possible. It opened my eyes to this whole new world of online entrepreneurship. I didn't realize you could use social media to make money. I thought it was just where you connected with your friends and kept in touch with people from high school.

My second one was with my first business. I thought after working with Mara that going into business would be simple and easy. In my first business, I modeled what saw working with Mara. I set up a collaborative blog where multiple experts could contribute to the blog. I did guest blogs on other people's platforms. I did a telesummit where I brought in other experts to speak. I gained a lot of visibility and became well known in that industry, but I wasn't making any money. It's not enough to get yourself out there. You must turn visibility into money by making offers. I wasn't selling enough. I was creating all sorts of free material, nurturing my customers, and creating visibility, but I wasn't making enough offers. I didn't have my paid offers or my profit pyramid figured out.

For my second business, I already knew how to build buzz, so all I focused on was selling. That's why I was able to hit $10,000 in the fourth month. I needed to sell and ask people to buy from me. Once I knew that, it became much simpler to make money.

Running the business was still complicated. It still felt like there were so many ways to build buzz and make offers. At the time, I was consuming so much information via webinars, PDFs, membership programs, and masterminds, and I felt that there was so much to do. It went back to feeling complicated. I was doing webinars, blogs, telesummits, Facebook ads, sales calls, live events, challenges, podcasts, and the list goes on and on. Every single person was teaching different things. I needed to organize it all, so I started sorting. What are all the strategies that people teach? How can I organize the strategies so they're systematic?

I realized that everything we learn and everything that's being taught by coaches falls into one of five categories: attract, nurture, convert, deliver, and operate. From there, it finally felt like I had a system and everything I created had a specific purpose. I could determine in which category each piece of content belonged. If you have a piece of content and try to do everything with it at once, it won't be as effective. Everything I created from that point became more focused and systematic.

> *Every single person was teaching different things.*

From there, as I was scaling up, I had to decide what I should do, and what I shouldn't do. I don't want to do all the things on the list. Within the categories, I started subcategorizing. Under attract, for example, which way of building your list feels hard and unsustainable and which feels scalable? I found that all the methods of attracting new customers fall into one of three subcategories: free, paid, and affiliate. Free is free, so that's why people typically start with it, but it's not scalable. It's a manual process. For paid and affiliate traffic, you can delegate or automate those processes, so those types are scalable.

I did the same thing for each category. The deliver step is a big one. I thought about all the things I could possibly offer. Which ones are hard, and which are easy and scalable? Under that, there are even more subcategories: active, leveraged, and passive income strategies. Active income offers would be one-on-one coaching, VIP days, or done-for-you services.

Leveraged offers are membership sites, group programs, or masterminds. Passive income includes do-it-yourself courses and software.

Where I'm Going

> *If we had to choose one high ticket offer to specialize in, what would it be?*

In Market Like a Nerd, we identified that the bulk of our clients' successes were coming from one specific thing: coaches starting to charge higher prices. From there, if we had to choose one high ticket offer to specialize in, what would it be? We chose masterminds because they deliver the biggest and easiest results. We are now tailoring our approach to just coaches, helping them to create, launch and scale their mastermind in our program, Sold-Out Masterminds.

As I mentioned before, I also joined forces with Jodi Sodini. She was one of my long-term clients who has been with me and I've been with her since the beginning of both of our businesses. When we met, she had one long-term client, but she was miserable and didn't enjoy that client. I told her I could coach her through it, fire him, and make more money. She hired me, fired the client instantly, and now is paying herself in the five figures monthly. Today, Jodi is my business partner. She originally had a done-for-you services agency, but now that Jodi is part of Market Like a Nerd, we will be offering done-for-you services in the future through the brand The Marketing Wonder Team. We'll be helping our clients implement their marketing plans.

> *We're about to launch something that I believe is the only service of its kind...*

We've been launching a $100,000 service through our higher-end clients where we are their chief marketing officers. That's been really fun. We also have some lower-ticket offers and services for people who aren't there yet.

We're about to launch something that I believe is the only service of its kind, a monthly cash injection management service, where we're implementing cash injection campaigns for clients every single month just like a marketing team would. We find that most virtual assistants just do what they're told; they aren't strategists and don't know how to make their clients money, so we're taking a very results-oriented approach in our done-for-you business.

To help scale our done for you business, we're going to need more people on our team. As the coaching business scales, we'll need more coaches to serve our clients. For that, we created a business called The League. In The League of Certified Coaches, we train other coaches on our material so that we can hire them to help our clients. The League of Certified Assistants certifies done for you service providers. Everyone we hire to serve our clients will be trained and certified by us. Of course, these coaches and virtual assistants will also be licensed, so even if we don't hire them on our team, they can go out on their own and use our material for themselves.

There are two other programs under Market Like a Nerd. One is a joint program with Yasemin Inal called the Brave Brigade, where we're supporting people more on their mindset. I've found in my work as a coach that mindset issues will come up. I'm a master of the marketing, but the mindset component is something that I recognized as a gap. Yasemin helps support the proper mindset, helping people to have the courage to do the things that they have to do in their business no matter how scary they are. Every entrepreneur is scared at some point. It was scary for me to leave my jobs at the age of 21 and become an entrepreneur. It was scary to hire my first coach at $12,000 per year when I grew up poor. It was scary to leave the business partnership even though we were making a lot of money and it was paying the bills when I had medical debt. It was scary to charge higher prices and launch my mastermind. It was scary to even let a business partner into my company. The Brave Brigade is helping people develop their confidence and the entrepreneurial mindset.

> *Every entrepreneur is scared at some point.*

The other program is the Endless Traffic Mastermind with Kimra Luna. This is for people who aren't ready to launch a mastermind yet, because they don't have enough traffic to support the launch. For newer entrepreneurs, the progression is the Brave Brigade to start with the right mindset, then the Endless Traffic Mastermind generates traffic and builds buzz, and then Sold-Out Masterminds helps you launch your high-ticket mastermind to the traffic that you've built.

Next year, I'm launching the first annual Coach-a-Palooza event, a festival and business conference. I envision it being high-vibe but quirky, with fun stuff like our event staff wearing staff capes like superheroes.

Besides that, I'm a Chief Marketing Officer in Del Grosso Law. She's also been a client from the beginning. I helped her build her business online which changed how much and how hard she was working. When I first met her, she was constantly on her phone, and now she's able to take a vacation and actually put her phone down. Her law firm is automated online with sales funnels, which is atypical for lawyers. We're now teaching other lawyers what we've done. It will turn more into a consulting agency for lawyers, to teach them how to scale and automate their businesses as well.

Another project is a software called the Coaches Secret Lair that helps coaches manage their clients. It's like a client management software for coaches where they can log call notes from their clients, assign tasks and reminders to their clients, track success and results in their programs, and generate statistics for their programs to show how effective their coaching is and to use for marketing materials.

Finally, Fame for Good is a branding and public relations agency I created with Minling Chuang that helps people to create aligned, creative authority brands.

I am multi-passionate and also love having multiple revenue streams. These various businesses keep me both happy and financially free.

> *I am multi-passionate and also love having multiple revenue streams.*

My Future Vision

I don't like to compare myself to others because I am my own person with my own talents, gifts, and abilities, but I imagine being like the next ClickFunnels, the female Russell Brunson. He has an amazing platform, a massive following with a massive event each year. He has massive impact, and there are not enough women who are doing things like that. If you ask people in our industry who their favorite millionaire mentor is, the answer is probably a man. It's time for a woman to step up to the plate.

EMPIRE BUILDER

AMANDA GOLDMAN-PETRI

After overcoming poverty, child abuse, rape, teen pregnancy, and near death, Amanda Goldman-Petri was able to persevere and grow five successful businesses by the age of 27. After perfecting her system, Amanda began her coaching career as founder of MarketLikeANerd.com, where she teaches coaches how to grow multiple 6-figure businesses without the hustle or sacrifice. After generating over half a million dollars in sales in 4 months and expanding her business to 31 different countries, Amanda became internationally renowned as the "Work Smarter, Not Harder" Online Marketing Coach.

While she was happy with her own results, Amanda realized true success as a coach is dependent on your client's results. She therefore shifted her attention to how she could make a bigger impact in her clients' businesses and lives. This led to her invention of a series of quick cash injection campaigns that her clients used to generate nearly a million dollars in sales in less than 60 days.

To access Amanda's gift, go to empirebuildersgift.com/bonus.

JODI SODINI

CONTRIBUTION

"Successful entrepreneurs have a vision for the contribution they want to make in the world. They see it on the horizon, focus on it and strive their entire lives to achieve it."

—Alex Charfen

When I was growing up in my small family comprised of just me, my sister, and my parents, I had NO idea that I would become an entrepreneur. Neither of my parents went to college and my sister started college but didn't finish. I was determined to be the first in my family to go to college and graduate, and so I did it. (Maybe that determination should have clued me into my entrepreneurial spirit!) After graduating top in my class with my EMT-Paramedic certificate, I went on to a thirteen-year career working on an ambulance; grueling 24-hour shifts would wear my mind and body out faster than I could have imagined. Apparently, the adrenaline rush wasn't quite enough because I also decided to become a firefighter while working full-time as a single mom.

> *I was determined to be the first in my family to go to college and graduate.*

When I met my now-husband, my career in EMS was about to come to a screeching halt. Unfortunately, his ten-year job did, as well. We found ourselves in the middle of the housing crisis in the U.S. while also experiencing major financial hardship and job loss… and I was pregnant. *WHOA.*

We both bounced between a few jobs and I took an office job as a Commercial Insurance Account Executive, but that didn't provide the steady income or the balance we needed for us to care for our family the way we wanted.

> *I had to figure out how to automate and scale my business quickly.*

I stumbled into a job at a brick and mortar virtual assistant company. Let me tell you, it didn't pay well, and I was working all the time. In my heart, I really wanted to work at home, be with my son, and not worry about the bills. Times were so tough that even with my husband working full-time, we were still struggling to make ends meet. Our lowest point was when we spent a month living in a borrowed camper. Essentially, we were homeless.

As luck (and gracious blessings from heaven!) would have it, my boss told me that people make money as VAs from home. I was floored. That would answer all my prayers. I decided I would learn how to build my own VA business and create one where I could both work at home and become financially independent. I took courses, hired business coaches, and basically dove head first into learning how to build a VA business. It was not without some challenges and special surprises. As I was starting up, we found out we were going to have another baby. I now had even more reason to make this business work.

Intuitively, I knew I had to figure out how to automate and scale my business quickly, so I learned as much as I could about social media marketing and automated sales funnels. After a lot of testing, hard work, and sleepless nights, I created an automated funnel that started bringing me consistent new leads for my business. Once I figured this out, I knew I was onto something. Soon my clients were asking me to help them create automated funnels too because they saw my success. That's when I realized that my business was more than a virtual assistant firm. We create custom-tailored digital marketing funnels and strategies that consistently get repeatable results.

I absolutely thrive on being in the trenches with my clients from around the globe, helping them strategize and craft their unique digital marketing funnels and strategy. I like to think of each step of our journey as entrepreneurs being another layer on the canvas. With each new layer we paint, it becomes a unique and brilliant piece of art.

As most entrepreneurs do, I have big plans and dreams to continue to grow and expand my business. I am not sure it's possible for me to feel "settled" or "done," so I continue to grow and expand. I recently downsized my team—from twelve subcontractors to six—in the name of focus and simplicity, and plan to keep this core team as is while my company brings in more revenue. We have found a niche of online coaches and consultants and have excelled at giving our clients a transformative experience by using digital marketing to scale their business to seven figures and beyond. I have heard the e-commerce niche call my name a few times and I'm feeling the urge to dabble in that, as well. We'll see!

My greatest desire, though, is to make a great contribution to the world. One of my mentors, Alex Charfen, says, "When looking at capitalism as a system based on the exchange of VALUE, those who make the greatest contributions tend to yield the greatest returns. These returns could be counted in money, but also in the personal fulfillment of changing the world for the better (money tends to be the most common measuring stick)." I want to support other online coaches, consultants, and change-makers so they can scale their business, create a massive impact, and make money while doing it. My client's success equals my success, meaning that

> *I have big plans and dreams to continue to grow and expand my business.*

I achieve my goal of making a great contribution to the world when I create transformational results for my clients!

The biggest lessons I've learned along my journey are:

Understanding that as entrepreneurs, we have an innate motivation. I know exactly when that kicked in for me (when I decided to start my own business). And it's more than a "desire" and it's more than "ambition." It's an intense FIRE burning inside of me that makes me capable of achieving anything. My family witnessed me become a different person.

My client's success really does equal my success, and my success also relies on my team being successful. When I worked as a solo service provider, I was the only one who created results for my clients. Now, my team creates the results along with me. So, I MUST have a solid team supporting me to be successful and create results for our clients.

I learn best through experiments and experiences. Yes, I can learn through books and consuming large amounts of data, but I don't feel the momentum of that learning if I don't get to apply what I learn through experiments and experiences. If this resonates with you...you MIGHT be an entrepreneur!

> *It's more than a "desire" and it's more than "ambition." It's an intense FIRE.*

Building a team is not easy. I've heard the phrase, "slow to hire, quick to fire" a LOT of times from coaches and consultants along the way. I didn't listen SEVERAL times and got burned more than once. I've had some duds on my team and allowed them to have second and third and fourth chances and, while I don't REGRET that, I'm not thrilled that I didn't learn a little faster.

When I invested in my business, my business grew by leaps and bounds. I remember hiring my first business coach, who is now one of my business partners in a separate venture. I was terrified of the investment, but my return on that investment was immeasurable. I invested with her 4 other times for coaching and other services and some of them were 5-figure investments! For example, I joined her mastermind at a cost of $12,000 for one year and my business transformed so much that I was making $12,000 per MONTH shortly after that investment. I'm not saying to go throw your money at any high-ticket coach and expect to get a big return and a transformed business. But I *am* saying that you won't get where you want to go alone. You need a mentor. You need a coach. The higher the cost, the more you are invested and committed to your business, and the higher your return. (Maybe I should have put a "warning: controversial statement ahead" here…)

> *The higher the cost, the more you are invested and committed to your business, and the higher your return.*

When I think over the past handful of years and all the clients that my team and I have served, I'm reminded of the results and transformations that we have created together:

We helped June successfully launch her Online Learning Platform and book with a live event in Washington, DC. (I've not facilitated any other live events and don't plan to, but it was fun!)

Rikka was able to focus more on being the CEO of her company while we supported her backend systems, resulting in major growth of her online business.

Joshua launched his first online program and we set up his entire website, opt in, and course platform so that he could make some serious bank!

My client Valorie has grown her FB page audience from 200k followers to 500k followers, we've improved her FB page engagement consistently, and have seen a to-date increase of 201%. Multiple FB ads are converting at 30%-40% (the average is 2%). We set up a free + shipping book funnel that has converted above average and with the faucet barely on, it's bringing in hundreds of dollars per week. Her live events have sold out 4x/year.

Kristi has been able to focus on bringing in more clients to her publicity firm while we take care of her Facebook group and her funnels that help her make passive income.

Mark has a brand-new website with a new visual brand that he is excited about and is much more pleasing to the eye than his previous outdated website.

> *You won't get where you want to go alone.*

We launched Angie's website and added an e-commerce store to sell her supplements. We built out her brand and overall web presence with setting up a podcast, doing more social media posts, and posting her blogs.

Jennifer had a 1-week launch of her online program and made over $500k. We helped build the opt in and sales pages, along with running all the paid traffic (Facebook Ads).

We built a full website on ClickFunnels for Jessica, after she had been let down by her previous VA. We also created a vLog and Podcast page for her on WordPress and connected the two sites seamlessly.

Minling has worked with us several times—for her telesummit and for other program launches. Her reaction to the sales page we created: "I didn't know that ClickFunnels could look like this!"

Tejal has a new passive income funnel (tripwire plus one-time-offer) that makes her money while she's sleeping (or growing a baby!).

Robin's shiny new funnel brings in about $1900/week with organic traffic.

Jennifer's new website allows her to get more credibility and trust from her potential clients and she's grown her business to being fully booked out in the past 2 years.

JODI SODINI

We have grown Facebook pages to over 10k likes (followers) for just $100 in ad spend.

We've been able to get $8 leads for a Realtor using Facebook ads (the average is $50).

Currently, we have seven more client funnels in the works and we anticipate several (at least three) of them hitting the seven-figure mark.

EMPIRE BUILDER

JODI SODINI

Jodi is a digital marketing genius and online business backend expert. The founder of BackendExpert.com and the new SignatureSocialAgency.com, she is known for turning the confusion and uncertainty that comes with an online business into streamlined systems and automation. This proud mom and wife has clients reporting major growth in their audience and their profits while spending exponentially less time on their business.

When you have so much on your plate that you're not even sure how to put it into words, Jodi can figure out what you need and deliver it.

To access Jodi's gift, go to empirebuildersgift.com/bonus.

VIDYA RAVI

YOU DON'T HAVE TO SEE THE WHOLE STAIRCASE, JUST TAKE THE FIRST STEP

This is not a rags to riches story—not exactly. I have not been in rags—like ever, and that makes it even more difficult when things go downhill. I will explain more in a bit.

Mine is more of a "You don't have to see the whole staircase, just take the first step" kind of story. Most of my life has been like that. I don't have sheets of papers planning my big goals with bridges around each goal. No, I had very few goals—mostly one or two at a time and I always took action on the first step I saw in my way.

> *I always took action on the first step I saw in my way.*

When I said I was never in rags, I mean my parents made sure that my brother and I had everything we needed as we grew up. I was a pampered child and also a straight-A student. I never left room for anything for my parents to complain about, at least in terms of my studies.

I was offered a job even as I started my last year of college. I was good at what I did, the job paid well, and I got great results.

Then, I met someone who I fell in love with and we got married. This was the first time things were different. I started to find a happiness, independence, and peace that were different than other parts of my life.

> *Eleven months after my baby boy was born, I went to my old job again.*

But, I also found that our financial situation became worse when we invested in a new home. When the baby came along, I wasn't able to work as steadily. That added to our stress. I wanted to be independent and help with our family's expenses. I was going mad and I didn't know what else to do.

I read a lot of fiction, around 800 books per year. For the first time, an author contacted me for publicity support. Different virtual book tour companies started hiring me and they said I could work from home. I broadened my horizons, and I started working for a couple of publishers.

The salary was still not enough to run our family with my student loan, car loan, and home loan. So, eleven months after my baby boy was born, I went to my old job again.

When Things Really "Blow Up"

If you are a parent, you already know how hard it is to manage your home and a job, with a toddler holding you every minute he is with you. It is hard to let go of the guilt; it's hard to tell your little one go find something else to play with and leave momma alone for a minute; it's hard to get a couple of minutes of breathing space when everything is moving so quickly and you find yourself never having time to do "anything," but you are still always working with as little sleep as possible.

That was another "hustle" day. I was cooking and my cab to the office would be arriving in 15 minutes. My son was holding my leg and I was walking around the kitchen with him grabbing me by the legs—I think I am not the only mom who does this.

We use an electric cooker with a whistle on the top to cook dhal. I was in a hurry and the cooker had whistled five times already. So, without realizing that the steam was still not reduced, I tried to open it. The cooker lid burst—*boom*, it literally blew off the top and I was covered in boiling dhal all over my face and body. The first thought I had was, "WHAT HAPPENED TO MY SON? HE WAS HOLDING MY LEG!" I was scared to death. I couldn't see him anywhere around me. I started crying and shouted for my husband. He ran towards me with our son in his arms and I cried in relief. I was so happy that he decided to go to his dad a few minutes before this happened.

Then I realized I had dhal all over me and it was burning my skin. Okay, yes, I cried again, and this time, it was for me. It was so painful. It was terrible and I knew I was not going to forget those boils any time soon.

I am that girl who shows up even when it's tough because I am needed.

So, we cleaned up and I had to go to the office anyway, so my husband dropped me off at the office a little late due to the accident. I was needed in the office that day, so I had to get there. Yeah, I am that girl who shows up even when it's tough because I am needed and I said I would be there.

Realization After the Universe Literally Poured Boiling Stuff in My Face

I can't forget how I felt when I feared my son could be somewhere in the kitchen when the incident happened. I was in tears even when I was at the office thinking of the things that could have gone wrong. Then it hit me.

I was doing this the wrong way. Yes, I wanted to support my family and I wanted to be independent, but I also wanted to be with my son. Isn't that why we had him in the first place? To be happy with him, to make memories and give him memories, to give the support he needs while he is growing up?

> *I was doing this the wrong way. I also wanted to be with my son.*

I made my decision. That night, I went to my husband and said I wanted to quit my job. He didn't look shocked, as I had felt when I made my decision. I tried to support my decision by saying "Hey, give me 3 months and I will make this work. I want to work online and do this for my sanity. I can't let these kinds of incidents happen ever again." This was the first time I took a step towards something that I didn't see where the whole staircase led.

I was surprised at what he said. He just said, "You never have to go back to your day job if you don't want to. I thought you liked your job. And you can try all you want for three months, and if that doesn't work, try another three months and then try again. I am always here and we will manage our bills somehow."

These were the exact words my dad said when we wanted to buy a home. When everyone else said it was a bad decision, when everyone else—both family and friends—were saying it was going to be so difficult, my dad said, "Just do it. You like it, right? Nothing else matters. I will always be here and we will manage." Even though I took my first step towards buying a new home, his words gave me the confidence that I could do it.

My younger brother said the same thing when I married my now-husband. All he said was, "Don't worry, I am here and we will manage." Without him, I would have been a big mess. I didn't know he had grown up until then.

I was so overcome by gratitude for the men in my life. The next day, I went to my office and said I want to quit. Everyone was stunned by what I said, because they were good people. I didn't have difficult bosses or colleagues. It was a difficult decision, but I said I had to quit for me.

My First Step Towards the Big Staircase...Which I Can't See in its Entirety Yet

I started as a tech virtual assistant and I was a natural. My client base grew consistently and some of them stayed with me to manage their entire marketing plans as I grew. Remember the three months deal? Well, I not only made it work, but I also doubled my day job income in three months. Yeah, I worked a lot, and I was obsessed to make it work.

There was a big learning curve in a short period of time and I loved that part of my world. I am clearly making an impact in my clients' businesses, while making an impact in mine.

Isn't that what the Universe guided me to do when it poured that boiling dhal over me?

It seems like it didn't. I am meant for more. I expanded my horizons and I tried different aspects of digital marketing to see what I loved most. I learned what I am great at.

> *I not only made it work, but I also doubled my day job income in three months.*

My Precious

The one thing I found myself attracted to was the results that I could get for my clients. I showed resourcefulness and was skilled in seeing the strategy for funnels and Facebook ads for a particular business.

That impact is what I hold as my success. That's "My Precious." When people say my ads created 5x ROI on their funnels, I don't just feel happy that it worked. I am also happy that they finally get to see what the right funnel and an excellent ad strategy can do.

If you haven't heard about marketing funnels, you should book a call with me. Funnels are how you work on your business and make your funnels work for you instead of you working for your funnels. This is not a pitch statement. If your funnels are not working like they should, you should see where the leaks are and fix them.

I realized some time ago that the energy I work with is very different than others. I don't just create funnels and ads; I also coach my clients along the way to make themselves an ideal client magnet. That's what worked for me and I wanted to have my clients' energy great too. That is one special thing that I bring to the way I work. I take care of their business health as well as their internal mindset health.

Do I See the Entire Staircase Yet?

No, I don't. But, I don't have to. I see my next few steps and I am happy with that.

> *Make your funnels work for you instead of you working for your funnels.*

You might wonder if I've ever taken a wrong step? Yes, of course, we all do. But, if you create enough support and guidance around you, you can make that advice the next step or make your next step the right one.

I created six figures in revenue the first year after I quit my job, and I am still growing every month. It's consistent growth and I feel loved and supported by my team and clients. I think I took a lot of right steps towards the top of the staircase.

It took a lot of hard work, learning, consistency, and dedication to get me here. Along the way, I realized I needed one more thing—the power of maintaining high energy and positivity "within" me.

There are so many people who showed me the light of the path along my staircase and also held me strong when I was about to fall. I am glad that I coach others who need that light along their steps. As I mentioned before, that's what makes me different. I combine energy and marketing together. Trust me, it meshes well.

> *I combine energy and marketing together.*

How about you? Are you ready for your first step? Would you like your first step to be the *right* one?

EMPIRE BUILDER

VIDYA RAVI

Vidya Ravi is the owner of VRDigital.co, a full-service digital marketing agency, specializing in funnels and Facebook ads. She holds an Engineering degree in Computer Science and is passionate about anything tech. With the support of her amazing team, and a super-amazing family, you can see her working her marketing magic on client products and services. When she is not working, you can find her cooped up with fantasy or romance novels or watching animated movies with her husband and son.

To access Vidya's gift, go to empirebuildersgift.com/bonus.

Katrina Hubbard

Stressed as Hell to Aligned AF

"If you can get the inside right, the outside will fall into place."

—Eckhart Tolle

Today, I write this chapter to you as the founder of Aligned AF, the magazine, mastermind and community for coaches, consultants and service experts who want to create an aligned, awesome as f+ck life and business.

Sounds like I must really have my shit together then, right?

But the reality is that only a short time ago: *I was what is now my perfect client.*

I was a stressed, burned-out service provider who wanted to all but jump the proverbial entrepreneurial ship.

I was successful on paper. But in reality...

I was drowning. Suffocating. Feeling like a failure.

> *No one knows what the hell **YOU** want.*

You see, all the business coaches, courses, and content in the world can provide you information, but no one is you. No one knows what will work for you. No one knows what makes you tick. No one knows what the hell **YOU** want.

Only you do. **And then again, maybe you don't.**

And that was me. I had no fuckin' clue. It took me hitting rock bottom to finally figure out that I've had it wrong all along.

Not just in business, **but, more importantly, in life.**

Allow me to explain...

You See, All My Life I Never Had a Real Direction

I always did whatever I *thought* needed to be done. I followed the prescription the adults wanted me to follow.

> *I knew I must be on the right track since I kept on winning.*

Be a gifted overachiever.

Take all the hard classes, and make all the A's.

Play all the sports, and win all the trophies.

Join all the clubs, and graduate with exceptional honors.

Looking back, I completed all this with no other intention than: This is what I'm supposed to do. This is how I will become successful. This is how I will make my parents proud.

And if I don't? I will be a failure.

That same fear of failure is what would later win me the local tennis "Heart and Hustle" award, after being diagnosed with mono my first day of class my junior year. Even though I was sick and tired, I still showed up. I still hustled my ass off to win. I still closed out high school with a 4.2 GPA, even though I could barely keep my eyes open in my junior year classes.

This was the beginning of my "hustle," my soon-to-be fifteen-year habit of blindly leaping from success to success, without taking care of myself or giving myself any real vision. There was a fire in me. Even though I didn't know what my direction was in life was, I knew I must be on the right track since I kept on winning.

I blindly gave my all.

I continued the parental prescription, and graduated from the University of South Florida with a Bachelors in Advertising at the start of the recession in 2009. I had a passion for creativity, and although I didn't get a design degree, I dreamed of one day being a rockstar art director in one of the major advertising firms they talk about in New York, California, and Colorado. You know, the ones who win all the creative awards, and work with all the Fortune 500 companies? The ones all wanna-be designers drool over? I wanted them drooling over my work. I wanted to be rolling in the moolah. I wanted to be living in a fancy high-rise condo and have the perfect husband.

It's the classic American dream: Climb the corporate ladder and get rich. Live the white picket fence lifestyle with the perfect family.

But everywhere I turned, people were getting fired. I couldn't even get an internship, let alone a career started. Hell, I couldn't even get a serving job in a restaurant!

A friend who lived in Dallas convinced me to move out there, since it looked far better on the economic front than Florida. Without knowing shit about what I was going to do, or where it was going to take me, I shoved whatever would fit into my car... And I drove.

For the first two months, I lived on the dining room floor of a couple's one-bedroom apartment. It was uncomfortable in that I knew the husband's nighttime pee schedule, as the only bathroom was five feet from where my head slept at night. I did luck out because my rent to be paid to them was having to play Dungeons and Dragons every week with their crew (although in full transparency, I'd rather stab my eyes out).

Two weeks into living in Dallas, I snagged a serving job at Carrabbas. I also hit up every agency in the Dallas Forth-Worth

> *It's the classic American dream: Climb the corporate ladder and get rich.*

Metroplex, begging for a design internship. ONE agency emailed me back. Four weeks into living in Dallas, I was granted a three-month UNPAID internship in design.

And so, the hustle went on. During the day, I worked my ass off for FREE in the agency world. At night, I made the only money I could as a server at Carrabbas.

Luckily, the unpaid internship was a success, turning into an almost 6-year agency career. I climbed the ladder from do-it-all intern, to production artist, to junior art director, to art director! The best part: they paid me to learn what most go to a design school and pay upwards of $100,000 to learn. AND for the icing, I was working on industry-leading brands.

This was it. Right? The whole point of following the prescription. I was living out *the* life.

Little did I know, I was slowly destroying it.

There's a type of unwavering loyalty you develop for a company when you lack any kind of vision for yourself. You lose yourself in the job. It's how you define yourself. It's how you start gauging who you *need* to be.

> *You lose yourself in the job. It's how you define yourself.*

When your boss strolls by your desk at 6:30PM and asks you to complete a last-minute client request, you grab some coffee, sit your ass back down at your desk, and you do that shit, even if you're left being in the office until 2AM to complete it.

After long enough, you start wearing the "work hard, play hard" persona like a badge of freakin' honor.

It's okay to work the 60- to 80-hour work weeks. It's how you'll keep getting better and continue climbing the corporate ladder.

It's okay to neglect sleep and spend your only free moments getting completely wasted with friends and co-workers, because this is free time. You've earned it.

It's okay to order out food consistently, exercise not at all and ignore your personal health, because when you've *made it*, THEN you'll have all the time in the world to focus on those little, less important things.

I learned how to hustle my face off for business and what I thought at the time was pleasure. It was a never-ending cycle that I ran for five freakin' years.

> *I sat there wondering what the point of it all was, to feel so horrible in the end.*

And then the inevitable happened.

Suddenly, I felt like the world was closing in on me. I started having bouts of difficulty breathing and tachycardia (a really fast heart rate). I started freaking the hell out. *What is wrong with me? Am I having panic attacks? Is there something wrong with my heart? Am I going to be okay?*

And then one night, I felt like I was replaying my past: I was just so sick and tired.

Tired of being sick and tired.

I had ordered my favorite heart attack meal from the local Italian restaurant. I sat there, creating the perfect imprint on my couch. I couldn't move. I just stared at the fish tank. Lifeless. Brain dead.

I felt defeated. I felt alone.

I had been so busy, running around with my head cut off, that there was no real time for building actual relationships.

I sat there wondering what the point of it all was, to feel so horrible in the end.

Then suddenly, I had a massive pain in my right side so sharp I yelped. I called my brother, freaking out. In a panic, he picked me up and rushed me to the hospital. They thought my gallbladder was failing me and it would be a rush surgery, but it turns out it was due to being overworked, over tired, stressed, and malnourished. Years later I would find the stress I brought upon my body had changed its chemical makeup, to the point where I could longer enjoy the same diet I once had.

After that, the fire that always burned inside me was gone. I no longer wanted to work hard, OR play hard. I simply wanted to do nothing.

I Stopped Everything

> *My entrepreneur self was born! VICTORY! I found my calling!*

Two weeks later, I quit my job. Two weeks after that, I quit my entire life in Dallas, and moved back to the Florida home I grew up in, with my parents.

What followed was a really strange year, a year of trying to "find myself" while I was half-ass looking for new agency jobs. Nothing appealed to me about it. In fact, nothing appealed to me at all.

I had been making decisions so blindly my whole life, I felt like I didn't know who I was anymore. If I didn't know who I was, how was I supposed to decide what I wanted?

Then one day, a friend of my mom's asked me if I could design her website. My entrepreneur self was born!

VICTORY! I found my calling!

Why should I have to work for someone else? NEVER. AGAIN. This is it! This will be the change I've needed all this time.

Fast-forward four years: **I woke up miserable.**

I had built the same bullshit life I had while I was at the agency. *I felt like the universe was playing a joke on me.*

But I faced the cold hard truth that this time: IT WAS NO ONE'S FAULT BUT MY OWN.

I was working the same hours, maintaining the same work hard, play hard, malnourished lifestyle. I was doing all the same things for myself that I had endured and that put me in the hospital! And I had no one to blame but MYSELF.

Even though I was following a new path, it was a similar path, just with a different label. Instead of being an employee doing anything to climb the ladder, I was now a small business owner, the entrepreneur who would do whatever it took to get to success.

This was my ULTIMATE wake up call.

I finally said to myself, overworked and overweight, "WTF, Katrina. It's time to stop this fucking bullshit!"

Eloquent, I know.

But that's why now, I stand here a changed woman. I have finally realized what it's all about. I must put myself first. I must know who I am, and **ultimately who I want to be**. I must create a life and business that aren't just balanced, but work in beautiful harmony. The moment you decide to be yourself, trust what you want, and not let the world dictate it for you—that's the moment the world will open up to you.

When you decide to have a vision, your successes will work in your favor.

When you blindly leap from success to success (or failure to failure!), without thinking about what it means to you, you can very easily wake up in a dark place, as I continued to do, so effortlessly.

You can wake up one day and realize that after all your hustle and hard-earned efforts, you built something you hate.

What do you do instead?

The answer comes down to this: Know who you are, and ultimately who you want to be. Then you can build your life around yourself to fit that awareness. This, my friends, is alignment.

> *You can wake up one day and realize you built something you hate.*

Now let me be clear: My life is by no means perfectly aligned. And quite frankly, no one's will ever be. Complete alignment is not something you can attain (and anyone who says otherwise is full of it). You never wake up and say, "Oh hey, I'm perfectly aligned today!", and then check alignment off your to-do list.

It is instead, the most incredible and exciting journey of self-discovery and self-actualization. It's knowing where you stand today, and how you can align your behaviors, thoughts, and emotions to anchor yourself to the version of self you want to become.

With every step I take, I am becoming more aligned. Each day, I am feeling more aligned.

My steps are now intentional. I'm working towards my vision. I'm giving myself purpose. I'm surrounding myself with people I love. And I'm giving myself permission to enjoy life to its fullest.

Without all the bullshit. Without all the hustle.

And so, I created my business, my movement, my passion: Aligned AF.

> *I've never been so happy to share what I do with others.*

And g'damn, I've never been so at peace with myself. I've never been so happy to share what I do with others.

I want to bring the journey of alignment in both life and business to other coaches, consultants, and service experts who are struggling to get to where they want to be, *just like I was.*

Even more, I want to help those who have never even asked these questions:

Who am I?

Who do I want to be?

I invite you to join me in the movement. I invite you to get Aligned AF, so you too can make those intentional steps towards the life you desire.

It all starts here.

I present you with a new prescription:

Questions to journal on, to get your own brain moving to learning what you want. The best part about this activity: There are no right or wrong answers! There is no failure. Only you, acknowledging and trusting in yourself.

We're going to look at seven categories of your life and decide what you want to create or experience in each of these categories.

Download and print out the worksheet, or just turn to a blank page in your notepad. Label the top of the page "What I Want." Take twenty minutes to write down what you would like to achieve in the next year, in each category of your life. Try to write down at least three things in each category (and even more if you've got 'em!). If you want, you can close your eyes and ask your subconscious mind to give you images of what your ideal life would look like if you could have it exactly the way you want it. Allow yourself to really visualize and feel into it. Then jot down those images for each of the following.

> *There is no failure. Only you, acknowledging and trusting in yourself.*

You may download the supporting "Aligned AF: What I Want" worksheet, which comes with an expanded audio for visualization support y visiting the Empire Builders bonus page at empirebuildersgift.com/bonus.

WHAT I WANT:

PERSONAL (Education, Spiritual Growth, Personal Development, Possessions, Experiences You Want)

....

....

....

FUN TIME + RECREATION (Fun, Vacations, Travel, Hobbies, Recreation, Sports)

....

....

....

HEALTH + FITNESS (Energy, Vitality, Strength, Flexibility, Weight, Hydration)

....

....

....

RELATIONSHIPS (Family, Friends, Colleagues)

....

....

....

CONTRIBUTION + LEGACY (Philanthropy, Volunteer Work, Community Impact)

....
....
....

BUSINESS (Projects, Location, Colleagues, Clients)

....
....
....

FINANCIAL (Income, Profit, Cash Flow, Net Work, Investments)

....
....
....
....

MAKE THEM GOALS:

Take those "wants" that you jotted down, and turn them into specific goals. How do we write a specific goal? By designating how much, by when. Think about how you would want to quantify each goal (i.e., Lose 10 pounds by December 31st).

Prioritize and take action on the "wants" that you wrote down. Do one thing per week in each of the seven areas that will get you closer to your goal.

Congratulations on finishing the "What I Want" exercise! From here forward, not only do you have goals for your dream lifestyle and business, but from now on, with every move you make, you can ask yourself THIS question:

DOES THIS ALIGN TO MY GOALS, AND WHERE I WANT TO BE?

If the answer is a HELL YES, have at it!

If the answer is NO, make it a pass, no matter if your decision disappoints others.

Remember: You are in control of your results!

BONUS: PERSONAL INSIGHTS + ACCOUNTABILITY

What was the most significant thing you learned during this exercise?

....

....

....

How did this exercise increase your self-awareness?

....

....

....

Why does this exercise matter to you?

....

....

....

What difference would following through on this exercise make in your life?

....

....

....

What would happen if I didn't follow through on this exercise?

....

....

....

Did you notice internal blocks that stopped you from fully participating?

....

....

....

Who can you ask to support you in accomplishing or holding you accountable to achieving your goals?

....

....

....

EMPIRE BUILDER

KATRINA HUBBARD

Katrina Hubbard is the founder and lead mentor at Aligned AF. Burned out in life and in business, Katrina realized she needed to get Aligned AF for herself. Now she's hell bent on sharing these life-changing truths, and can't wait to see others thrive.

To access Katrina's gift, go to empirebuildersgift.com/bonus.

CONCLUSION

*I*f you're anything like me, now that you've read the book you're probably full of great ideas for your business. Before too much time goes by, please visit empirebuildersgift.com/bonus to download the free gifts from the authors.

We'd love to see you in our closed Facebook Group, Empire Builders, to connect with like-minded female entrepreneurs and interact with the book contributors at https://www.facebook.com/groups/302300036955100/.

www.ingramcontent.com/pod-product-compliance
Lightning Source LLC
Chambersburg PA
CBHW021956290426
44108CB00012B/1099